E

MW01492753

From Jason Albelo, Lead Pastor
East Hill Church Family

Murl Silvey has an incredible grasp of the emotional development of human beings. Murl does an incredible job of coupling the emotional development of human beings with the Christ-centered biblical insights that pour right from Scripture. I have found Murl's insights not only helpful as a pastor and leader of a church but also as a shepherd of my family. Having heard and used the insights contained within these pages, both personally and professionally, I am confident that you will be stretched and blessed through the material that follows. If you are leading in any capacity, then read carefully and take notes. The information you are about to encounter will not only greatly enhance your perception of spiritual and emotional formation for yourself but also give you a keen perception of how to identify, assess, and improve the spiritual formation of those whom you serve.

From Dan George, Pastor

Dr. Murl Silvey is a gift. His wisdom and insight and teaching methods have profoundly impacted my personal and professional life. He is that rare combination of both developmental psychologist and biblical scholar. This unique blend has afforded him a significant vantage point to see the deeper needs of human beings to grow and develop in emotional and spiritual maturity. His genuine personal warmth and compassion open the door for his students, patients, and the leadership groups he teaches to walk through where the real discovery, learning, and personal growth take place. After thirty-two years as a husband, father, and pastor, Dr. Silvey stands out as one of the truly wise men that I have known in my life. I am grateful to recommend his book; you will be rewarded for reading it.

From Lesa George

The SOCA process gently, lovingly, and without judgment facilitates in identifying the "whys" we might be cemented and wedged in the memories of the past or accommodating for the future so that we miss out in the joy-filled living of today. With each of the SOCA principles prayerfully applied comes a freedom, a happiness of knowing that God made you unique and wonderful, and a thoughtfulness of being forgiven, loved, and understood so that you, in turn, can show and encourage others. This has helped me dismantle the walls that I had carefully fabricated and fortified to keep my motives from being understood and my pain from being felt. It teaches how to get a thoughtful heart while keeping compassion in mind. Dr. Murl and Bev Silvey have first and foremost lived what they believe and then, by example, have been the kindest mentors. I have clearly seen and witnessed Jesus through them. They helped me transform my expectations into hope!

From James L. Born, PsyD

Murl Silvey became my fellow spiritual pilgrim, professional colleague, mentor, and friend when he invited me to join Mt. Hood Counseling Service in Sandy, Oregon, seven years ago. I know Murl Silvey as a compassionate, dedicated clinical psychologist who is informed by his Judeo-Christian values and worldview, to the change, growth, and development of the personal "self." By integrating concepts of psychology and spirituality, he has synthesized basic life principles, which point a person in the direction of "emotional interpersonal maturity development" (EIMD). These principles commence with an unfolding of the concept of "what is the self". Using a seven-stage EIMD paradigm, the person looks non-judgmentally at self, into this paradigm's mirror, to consider one's own emotional development.

Next, how a person changes/grows/develops one's self-reflection needs four essential tools: self-observation, other-person perspective, consequential thinking, and alternative thinking. Having gathered information, considered the possibilities, and discerned the obstacles, the person determines a plan of action which will facilitate their growing in peace and contentment with who they are, with whoever they may be at the time, with whatever circumstances they may be experiencing. The key is what a person's "self" reflects. For what a person focuses on is what they become and what the individual will reflect.

His book is a must-read for any professional psychologist, counselor, therapist, minister, or chaplain who seeks an approach to counseling that integrates psychology and spirituality. In addition, the book is written in a manner that the general reader can understand and benefit from in the quest for emotional interpersonal maturity development.

From Morgan Katherine Hjelm, MDiv, AACC Certified Counseling Minister

This book is vital to the growth and maturity of people who wish to find peace in life. The program in this book changed the lives of our entire family. Three generations learned this program. The instruction is flawless in teaching responsibility for feelings and behavior. Peace and freedom come with understanding that I cannot be someone else's problem, because we can choose our feelings. What I've experienced is that if the epiphany occurs; the person's life is truly changed for the better, and unresolved issues are resolved quickly. As a counseling pastor I will use this book in our church and hopefully throughout the denomination.

From Mike Vermace, Pastor and Chaplain

Having known Dr. Silvey for a few years now and hearing his heart for healing and for individual healthy and spiritual maturity, it is exciting to see this book has come to fruition. Dr. Silvey's Four Requirements for Development (Self-Observation, Other-Person Perspective, Consequential Thinking and Alternative Thinking) are important for everyone to understand, and his ability to clearly explain the thoughts and concepts involved makes them more than understandable. These developmental pieces help each of us see how we are both "wired" and blessed by God. Dr. Silvey's ability to reveal this to others will help people develop healthy boundaries in life and maturity. Bottom line: this book will help get people "unstuck." Way to go, and thank you, Doc!

MATURING
IN
CHRIST

A Lifetime Journey

Murl Silvey, Psy. D. and
Bev Silvey, MA

WESTBOW®
PRESS
A DIVISION OF THOMAS NELSON
& ZONDERVAN

Unless otherwise noted, all Scripture quotations are taken from the New International Version (NIV) as found in *The NIV Study Bible, New International Version* (Zondervan Bible Publishers, 1973, 1978, 1984, 1985).

All Scripture quotations marked (NASB) are taken from the *New American Standard Bible*, copyright 1960, 1962, 1963, 1968, 1971, 1972, 1973, 1975, 1977, 1995 by The Lockman Foundation. Used by permission. All rights reserved worldwide.

WestBow Press books may be ordered through booksellers or by contacting:

WestBow Press
A Division of Thomas Nelson & Zondervan
1663 Liberty Drive
Bloomington, IN 47403
www.westbowpress.com
1 (866) 928-1240

ISBN: 978-1-4908-6738-0 (sc)
ISBN: 978-1-4908-6739-7 (hc)
ISBN: 978-1-4908-6737-3 (e)

Library of Congress Control Number: 2015901103

Print information available on the last page.

WestBow Press rev. date: 02/26/2015

CONTENTS

This book is dedicated to Murl's mother, Evelyn Silvey, who represented true inspiration of love and growth in Christ. Even in differences she would encourage others in love so that Christ was magnified.

Steven Sauter was the key editor of this book. He spent many, many hours writing and rewriting the information I presented to him. He gave a creative narrative to the book. Without Steve's commitment to the material and his own growth in the process, this book would not have been published.

To the brave women and men who have worked diligently and courageously on their life journey, overcoming past traumas, developing healthy self-observers, expanding their other-person perspective, and learning how to be effective in relationships.

PREFACE

I have always been interested in how people develop and mature. Over the years, I have read a lot of material and developed some of my own material that has been very helpful in my practice. The research that my therapeutic style is based on holds great promise for those seeking answers for their own growth; however, today the original research is almost entirely lacking in the current literature and therapeutic practice. In light of the value of these concepts, I decided it was time to reach beyond my practice to the wider audience a book might provide.

As I started writing, I also did a thorough review of the current literature to see if somewhere the principles that I have taught for so many years are still in print. My search confirmed what I suspected: there is a void when it comes to this particular researched perspective on personal growth. The search also confirmed that human need has not changed.

Here are some of the things that I found when I went online to see what others have written. A site on spiritual leadership called "Spiritual Maturity and Its Importance," by Dr. Richer Krejcir, included research conducted between 1996 and 2001 of various church leaders. The overall conclusion was that more than 80 percent of church leaders surveyed were satisfied with the way they were. The survey also revealed that churches were not challenging their members to a deeper growth. Instead of moving deeper into what Christ desires, they focused on something they felt needed to be fixed—in other words, Band-Aids as a substitute for major surgery. Of the pastors surveyed, 81 percent indicated that there was no regular discipleship program or effective effort of mentoring members or teaching them to deepen their Christian foundations at their church. Barely 20 percent sought real answers. Complacency reigns in the church.

Research between 2002 and 2007 indicated that almost two-thirds of church members do not have an accurate view of the Bible and are not challenging themselves to personal spiritual growth. A recent poll in France showed that 89 percent of the people polled admitted that they needed something to give life meaning.

Viktor Frankl, in *Man's Search for Meaning*, said, "Suffering ceases to be suffering in some way at the moment it finds meaning." Today people are desperate to find meaning in their suffering but find answers elusive. The rigid structures we construct for ourselves are often too limited or restrictive, and Christians find themselves in needless distress.

Most people, especially Americans, would consider being happy an important goal. Christians take this a step further, "After all that Christ has done for me; I of all people should be happy and joyful all the time." Like some unwanted disease, unhappiness is seen as a telltale symptom of a contagion that a Christian shouldn't have, so it is easy to be ashamed of feeling unhappy. For the Christian, there are many opportunities like this to misunderstand who God is and who we are; the result is often compounded suffering.

When a belief system conflicts with a person's basic needs, life begins to lack meaning. No wonder many people are hurting and feel they have nowhere to turn for answers. They want to blame someone or something, often God. Even those who hold a God-based belief system can feel terribly isolated, wrestling with life's deepest questions. For years, Christians who are suffering and feeling that God cannot be found anywhere have touched me. These are some of their cries:

- "If you are real, God, enable me to understand you or feel you enough so I am convinced you really care for me."
- "Why should I believe you when I look at what happens at church?"
- "God, I am so mad at you! It makes me want to say I don't care anymore."
- "I was sexually abused at church, and you did not protect me."
- "God, why did you let it go on so long?"
- "How do I know that you will be patient enough with me to let the real me change, not just the me I've been told you want?"
- "I'm so scared that you don't really love me. There's no hope for anything different."
- "God, take me, not my child; let her live."

Hearing these cries of anguished hearts is not surprising to me, as I have been working with churches, church leaders and people from churches for more than forty-five years. These cries for help and meaning, combined with the stark nature of the research, have motivated me to compile and publish. It is a great burden on my heart and, I think, on the Lord's heart as well to bring assistance to His church.

The design of this book is meant to be both informational and practical but most of all usable. I have included many explanations of the important pieces to help you identify where you are on your own personal journey toward Christian maturity. Included are practical activities and exercises for exploration and suggestions of where to turn for assistance and how to tackle some of the more thorny issues that we often encounter as we seek answers, meaning, and moving forward. I strongly encourage you to answer the questions at the end of each section. You can complete them either by yourself or in a group.

Please do not use any of this material to judge others or to be critical toward them. This also includes criticism toward oneself as the reader. It is often painful to view areas of deficit if your upbringing shamed you for this. My encouragement for you is to observe and not judge yourself or others in the growth process outlined in what follows. Remember, God told us not to judge (Matthew 7:1).

This material is a tool to look at ourselves and to work on the lifelong process of developing Christlikeness. It is also helpful in providing understanding of others by thorough insight from their words and actions. By looking at others through the eyes of our Lord Jesus, we can see them and ourselves completely differently, unconditionally loved. I pray that God will use these tools to develop mature Christians, bright lights in a dark world. (As Matthew 5:14 says, "You are the light of the world.") In turn, as we develop toward maturity, we will find ourselves mentoring others to more Christlikeness.

My mother, Evelyn, did not know all the psychological terminology of SOCA, but she was certainly aware of others around her. This awareness led her to caring, giving, and empathic actions towards others. Where did she learn these skills and obtain these insights? These ways of relating to others, really listening and observing, came from loving relationships within her own family and circle of friendships.

My wife Bev's personal growth is a tribute to very hard work on her part. Bev enjoys caring and giving to others and will share her creative ideas and knowledge freely. Both these women are gifted in their insights, and I am most fortunate and enriched that they are a part of my life. Very different backgrounds have resulted in two women with great maturity. The message in Bev's background is one of great hope, central to the intent of what follows in this book. Our background does not need to determine our future relationships or maturity, and that change is not only possible, it is God's heart desire for each of us to grow up in Christ.

For those who didn't have the kind of modeling I had (some of whom are reading this book right now), who came from horribly dysfunctional families instead of showing healthy ways to relate and interact, there is good news. There is hope and a positive future.

Everyone can learn new patterns of relating. My clinical practice has been dedicated to bringing this learning into the lives of my clients. I have seen countless individuals who rose above their life's circumstances and learned new and healthy ways to see themselves and improve their abilities to relate well to others.

It probably goes without saying that our society grows more and more confused as it loses its way. It is God's desire that the church rise as a beacon of hope and light as the world swirls into the dark—that the church would possess the answers to life's hardest questions, show the way to wholesome interactions, and open the door to peace with God. Unfortunately many in the church have lost their way as well. The statistics paint a sad picture of complacency, and the truth is that many individuals are not finding the assistance and guidance that the church is designed to provide. Instead of providing meaning for the suffering they encounter in the world, many churches have been the source of suffering for some of their members. It does not need to be this way.

My clients have told me that they often feel I care for them in our sessions. I believe this is because I demonstrate what Christ does for me. He hears me, He understands me, and He cares for me. This simple summation of human need is what He longs to be for you.

I would like to invite you into my office. I sit in a well-worn reclining office chair; you may sit in the much-loved leather chair or on the couch. This invitation is not actually to be my client but to enter a place of safety and caring as you read. I desire for you to know that this place of safety I have described is a small reflection of the height and the depth of the love that God has for you in Christ Jesus! He will be with you as you pursue your journey.

Viktor Frankl wrote, "Unconditional Love is, the ability to see the essential traits of a person and even more, that which is the potential". Loving someone unconditionally allows them to develop their strengths and continue to grow.

It is my prayer and desire that you will feel this unconditional love and find that in Christ you are able to reach your greatest potential, freed from your darkest cell, and discover the peace and joy that is God's heart for you.

CHAPTER 1

INTRODUCTION TO SOCA
SELF-OBSERVER, OTHER-PERSON PERSPECTIVE
CONSEQUENTIAL THINKING,
AND ALTERNATIVE THINKING

Because it cannot be seen, many ignore their inner world and say that if it exists, it isn't important. They claim, "You can certainly get along fine without it," but from this perspective, when things go wrong, it is very difficult to know what to do. As you know from your car or any other object of internal complexity, it is impossible to fix without an awareness of the mechanisms and logic of its construction.

We can easily see a broken arm or other external bodily injuries; yet the inner mind and soul are often neglected. We seek help in repairing our physical bodies, yet we fail to seek understanding, insight, and awareness of our internal processes. God made us complex, very complex, and we need to develop understanding into our deepest heart, soul, and strength. As you develop into maturity, you can learn to monitor your own internal world, the pulse of your emotions, the fever heat of your anger, and the soothing calm that comes from insight into your feelings, insight that leads to freedom of choice.

You can choose to express your emotions rather than become your emotions, to feel wind but not be carried away by it.

This is foundational; everything else is built on the foundation stones like the building of a church. Without the foundation the building will collapse. Spend time learning these four foundational elements in development.

Four Essential Growth Areas for Development

1. *Self-Observation*—An awareness of one's own thoughts, feelings, and behavior. This includes self-examination of one's own motives, desires, and habits. It is a process over time of recognizing the uniqueness of how God made you, distinctively you! Self-observing is an awareness of your likes and dislikes, of your mind's thinking patterns, of the inner conversations you have with yourself. God created in you a beautiful mind of reasoning and reckoning. How well do you know your thoughts? How often do you ask yourself, "How am I feeling?" How do your thoughts and feelings affect your behaviors? Without understanding your internal self, how will you know the uniqueness with which God created you? This awareness will begin simply and proceed to richer understanding of who you are in Christ. I invite you to begin your self-observer awareness journey; "… and we take every thought captive to make it obedient to Christ" (2 Corinthians 10:5).

2. *Other-Person Perspective*—An awareness of the other person's thoughts, feelings, and behaviors. Other-person perspective involves a growing awareness of another's point

of view. It requires that you develop compassion, empathy, and understanding of and for another person. People need to be heard, understood and cared for from birth to death. Part of other-person perspective is learning to recognize that other individuals might not think, feel, or choose actions the same as you would. We are all uniquely made. We all have different past experiences that affect the present. Learning to follow the scripture, Matthew 19:19, "love your neighbor as yourself," is imperative to developing other-person perspective.

3. *Consequential Thinking*—A consideration of the benefits and negative consequences if a certain action is taken. Consequential thinking reflects on the outcome before the action and evaluates the correctness of reasoning. How will my actions affect my life as well as those around me? Are my actions conveying God's grace and love; or are they full of impatience and mistrust? Developing advanced thinking skills before the action will ease the frustration and pain of having to seek forgiveness for things you did not mean to say or do in the first place. Consequential thinking can be thought of as a safety measure for life's journey.

4. *Alternative Thinking*—The process of brainstorming ideas or potential options. We need to develop the ability to find alternative options of choice and make different choices in order to avoid being stuck in a pattern of behavior that keeps us from growing on our life's journey. There is a wealth of alternatives for every choice. We need to develop the ability to weigh the consequence of each choice and to make the best decision at the time. As you are developing alternative thinking, use the resources of wise counsel from another

person. Your skills will increase as you have success in choosing effective alternatives.

After we have covered SOCA in detail, next we will look over the Seven Stages of Development in detail. There will be lots of questions to ask yourself so that you can identify which stage you might be stuck in and how to move forward in the journey.

Then we will reveal common hindrances that profoundly affect our spiritual growth. These hindrances also affect our relationships, our jobs, and our ability to communicate with others as well as our ability to grow through the stages. There will be lots of questions for you to ponder and journal about. Along this journey we will suggest tools that might be helpful for you to implement.

Stay with us; don't get discouraged or give up. We know you can do this because through Christ Jesus our Lord we can be strengthened and do all things.

CHAPTER 2

THE S IN SOCA
Self-Observation

"Gentlemen, this is a football." Vince Lombardi

Like football, some things in life are all about the basics, no matter how expert we are or think we are. If we overlook these basics, we do so to our harm and the harm of others. When properly employed, they can be of enormous good for our growth and for those we love.

Of these basic skills, nothing is more fundamental than the *S* (self) in SOCA. It is difficult to overstate the power of objectively observing one's self. The simple act of self-observation is a wrecking ball for the dilapidated constructs of our pasts, and it is the first play in the game in developing the new "us" we long for so much.

Self-Observation and Becoming a Self-Observer

From Scripture you are encouraged to "take every thought captive" (2 Corinthians 10:5) a major step in becoming an effective self-observer.

Self-observation is the term I use to describe an awareness of one's own thoughts, feelings, and behaviors. This includes examination of one's own circumstances and being objective about what is seen. Those who are developing self-observers are more able to grow and develop into the persons God desires them to become. Self-observing can lead to an individual developing into a mature and Christ like Christian. A self-observer is someone who has learned the art and practice of noticing and questioning. "Why do I react this way, think this way, or treat others in this way?"

Why Develop Self-Observation Skills?

Many adults rationalize what they do or say with unproductive statements such as "Well, that's just who I am." In reality they don't have a clue who they are. Why? Because the first and most important step in knowing one's self is taken through self-observation. It is the most essential of all areas for development. Without this capacity, staying stuck is likely. Without observation, the tools required for maturity are out of reach.

The total lack of self-observation, in its purest form, can be seen in an infant. Whether by smile, wail, or piercing scream, every impulse is instantly registered without regard for day or night or the disruption caused to either parent. A young child also does not self-observe, acting purely on impulse, a slave to feelings. How many adults still fit this description? Do you still find yourself here?

And so we have a society that is increasingly impulse-driven, wanting instant and continuous gratification. We are a culture of many distractions from developing a healthy self-observer; there are always movies, games, drugs, sex, pornography, shopping, gossip … a myriad of things to occupy the mind with everything and anything but that one thing that leads to the better man or woman God desires and is calling each of us to become.

Many adults find themselves confused by the failure of their marriages, relationships, and jobs. They wonder why their children hate them and don't listen to them and why their wives or husbands are leaving them. They weren't able to read the clues. Be assured, there is hope for understanding and change!

The capacity for self-observation begins in the teen years. However, capacity does not equal productive implementation. *Insightful, mature*, and *circumspect* are not the words most parents would use to describe their teenagers. It is a time of tremendous relational experimentation and therefore a good time to introduce the concept of self-observation. I have seen individuals who choose to change be enormously helped by the basic concept of self-observation. How does this unfold and become incorporated into our daily lives? As with many skills, growth and change come with effort and practice over time.

> Linda sat staring. She was angry to be in a therapist's office, angry that her life was a mess, and angry that her family and friends and co-workers were angry with her. They had ample reason to be angry with her, but she couldn't see it. "How did I get here?" was her question to me and to herself. As we worked together, she began to see and take responsibility for the damage her razor-sharp tongue and quick temper were causing in her relationships. Initially it was a long time after the fact that the mental sorting out of

what had happened in her relational skirmishes. As she continued to work, the whole process began to condense, till one day she was able to self-observe right in the middle of an argument! She celebrated that day and continues to progress in self-observing before speaking or taking action. It's changed her life.

In saying things they wish they could take back and taking actions that cause deep harm and regret, most adults follow a pattern similar to Linda's: they self-observe after the fact. And if that's where you find yourself, that's where you start. With work, the process of learning to observe moves awareness from closer to the moment at hand to being in the moment and finally to before the moment.

Learning to Observe without Condemning
Why Is It Important to Be Objective about Yourself?

Would you agree that you want to have valuable and meaningful relationships? Are you willing to work through change so that you might enjoy these relationships? Self-observation is one of those valuable lessons that will bring about change and better relationships. Feelings of shame, guilt, and personal condemnation are warning bells that an individual has slipped into self-judging, and self-judging usually dead-ends the observation process for any useful and constructive use.

Steve reflects on a conversation that he has with a friend. The conversation ends abruptly with Jeff hanging up on him. As Steve replays the conversations in his mind, he recalls where he interrupts Jeff and tells him that he's wrong three times immediately prior to the dial tone. Steve feels bad; the introspection is painful because it always results in him being self-condemning and shame filled. He stops self-observing; it's just too painful.

***

From another: "There you go dredging up our trip to Europe again. That has nothing to do with us right now," Trina shrilled. "The only reason I brought it up was because you said the same thing in Europe, as you are now," Brian said softly. "Every time I bring up how you are hurting me, you say that makes you feel like a bad person. You said it in Europe, and you just said it again now. I've never called you a bad person. What is it that's keeping you from hearing what I'm really saying?"

The goal in self-observing is to be objective. Objectivity is the distinguishing trait of the strong observer; this balance unlocks beneficial insights to both the positive and the negative aspects of thoughts, feelings, and actions. It is like becoming a dispassionate third party in your observation, gleaning a crime scene for any information that can provide useful or helpful insights in order to solve "the problem." This is considerably different from seeing yourself as "the problem," which may occur when objectivity is lost. Insight allows the strong self-observer to learn to acknowledge and express the full range of feelings, from caring and loving to anger, bitterness, or rage, and yet not allow these feelings to take over control. You can have your feelings without becoming them.

The Self-Observer Spectrum

Individuals who choose to embark on the self-observation exploration can look for growth markers along the way. What follows are some of those markers, moving from more basic to greater growth and toward maturity. Note that these markers are both consecutive and cumulative. Mature observers add these skills and mind-sets as they grow.

Observing Closer to the Moment at Hand: Awareness/Mindfulness

The goal in self-observing is to be able to step outside of yourself and your circumstance and view what is seen with the objectivity of a third person, to be aware of thoughts, feelings, and behavior and to take into account the thought process and how feelings and actions are interacting in relationship with people and circumstances. For many people it is only after they have calmed down after an argument that they can observe past action or consider what they said. It is okay to take an adult time-out and consider what has happened. Ask yourself the question, "What could I have done differently in this situation?"

Observing in the Moment: Deepened Observations Coupled with Changing Behaviors

As the self-observer strengthens, the ability grows for greater development and to recognize when progress has stopped. You begin to see when you are stuck. The capacity exists to measure progress in times of positive growth as well as take an inventory and accurately assess when regression is occurring. Then determine what needs to change to move back into a path toward developing maturity. Now I can stop in the middle of saying something, pay attention to how what I said might sound to the other person, and then restate it again more clearly.

Observing before the Moment: Growth Style

An individual who has developed a self-observing style of growth can identify what needs to change and then make a plan, including and initiating steps to change one's own thoughts, feelings, and behaviors. This includes examination of motives, desires, and habits. Foresight is also a characteristic of "before the moment"—anticipating and predicting what an interaction or circumstance may yield, based on what you have previously experienced, and preparing appropriately. People at this stage are far less likely to use statements such as "I had no idea that she felt this way" or "Dennis really blindsided me with the office restructuring plan" or "I thought the kids were happy at their new school. How was I to know?" Individuals who are progressing through this stage of observation can hear what is being said in their mind and can evaluate the conversation and clarify what is the best way to answer, not just react before observing.

Self-observers can find personal congruity, honesty, and integrity within their own selves. As the inner observing strengthens, they will continue to change and develop in relationships towards a healthy interaction.

God's Desire: Process and Presence

God desires your growth. He has laid its process out and He promises to be present with you in supporting the changes you will make. God has given us scripture that invite us into action to be all that God wants us to be. Some of these scriptures follow:

- "A man ought to examine himself ..." (1 Corinthians 11:28)
- "Examine yourselves to see whether you are in the faith; test yourselves." (2 Corinthians 13:5)
- "Surely he recognizes deceitful men; and when he sees evil, does he not take note?" (Job 11:11)
- "We demolish arguments and every pretension that sets itself up against the knowledge of God, and we take captive every thought to make it obedient ..." (2 Corinthians 10:5)

By using scripture as an evaluating road map, the self-observer can see change as a positive and God-given opportunity to continue developing and growing toward the individual that God has designed each of us to be. The best part is that He promises to be with us in the process, not only "to will and to do His good pleasure" but "Lo, I am with you till the end of the age" (see Philippians 2:13; Matthew 28:20).

Learning to listen, observe, and understand can have initial pitfalls. For example, have you ever listened to your recorded voice or watched a video in which you appeared? Perhaps just asking this question causes you to become a bit uncomfortable.

"It does that for me," explained one of my clients. "I don't enjoy listening to or hearing myself. I wince at my mistakes and awkwardness; I'm so uncomfortable I don't learn much from what I see. The same is true for learning to observe myself in interactions with others as well as observing my thinking and behavior. It was hard to look carefully at myself without condemning; sticking with my observing was just too painful. Because of this I didn't grow much at first."

Imagine this personal growth process with God walking step by step with you. What an awesome picture that creates. Well, guess what: He is carrying you along the pathway in this journey. Remember that God loves you completely and is not the source of either shame or condemnation. If you begin to experience this as you reflect or journal, stop to reaffirm what is true about you because of your standing in Christ, and then invite Christ to walk with you.

Many memories are painful to revisit, and I would like to draw a distinction between shame and pain. Inviting Christ to walk with you and bringing the shame to Him when it does come up will be helpful in dealing with the pain of shame. Christ also suffered and is with you when you dip into a valley. He promised that if you invite Him and expect Him to walk along with you in this process, He will be there.

Self-Observer Questions to Ask Yourself

These questions are designed to guide and awaken your awareness in your ability to self-observe. Take time now either in conversation or with a journal to reflect on the following.

1. Can I be objective about myself, recognizing my own biases?
2. Do I search for meaningful insights into my thinking, actions, and patterns of behavior and at the same time notice if I am becoming personally condemning?
3. Can I love myself while at the same time recognizing my sinfulness and weaknesses?
4. Can I be conscious of my thoughts before they become an impulse-driven direction or an action, or do I find myself wondering how things went so wrong in this conversation, business deal, or relationship?
5. When I experience a feeling, am I able to be constructive with that information, or am I prone to overreact? In other words, am I informed by my feelings, or do I tend to become my feelings?
6. Can I observe my actions and behavior and use this information to avoid impulsive reactions, choosing my desired direction?
7. Can I recognize and acknowledge my personal limitations and issues without being critical or judgmental of myself?
8. Can I accept my physical limitations and abide within them, while making efforts to improve my physical well-being—and all without giving up or pushing beyond these limitations so that I end up injured?
9. Can I have a positive attitude toward the future when the circumstance in the present is very difficult and demanding?

10. Can I look at my past decisions and actions, taking responsibility without judgment that leads to guilt and shame?
11. Can I love others in a godly way without projecting my own biases and feelings on them?
12. Do I evaluate my motives for doing things before I do them? Do I stop and ask myself, "What is my motivation for doing this?" before I agree to do them?
13. Can I manage my strong feelings so that I don't say or do something that will hurt others or myself?
14. Do I let other people or circumstances influence me too much?

Before proceeding to the next section, spend some time breathing and relaxing. When you are ready, reflect on the following:

a. What does this mean to you, "to be a beloved child of the Father"? You are a child of the Most High King; do you believe this?
b. In what ways does this statement apply to you: "There is therefore no condemnation for those in Christ Jesus our Lord"? Jesus Christ has paid the price. Allow His grace and forgiveness to cover you during your life process.
c. Am I able to align my view of self with God's view? "God loves you, God is love." You mean so much to God the Father; you are precious, chosen, and forgiven before Him.

For years I have urged clients to remember than any thought or feeling can take you further than you want to go, keep you longer than you want to stay, and cost you more than you want to pay. With time, as you develop the Self-Observer, you will be able to consider whether a thought or feeling is from the flesh, from the world, from spiritual adversaries, or from the Holy Spirit.

As you read the Bible on a regular basis, you will be able to see yourself through the different individuals in the Bible and through the Holy Spirit, who will speak into your life the areas in which you need to develop further.

Self-Observer Scriptures

My son, if you accept my words
    and store up my commands within you,
turning your ear toward wisdom
    and applying your heart to understanding,
and if you call out for insight
    and cry aloud for understanding
and if you look for it as for silver
    and search for it as for hidden treasure,
then you will understand the fear of the Lord
    and find the knowledge of God. (Proverbs 2:1–5)

Everyone ought to examine themselves before they eat of the bread and drink from the cup. (1 Corinthians 11:28)

We demolish arguments and every pretension that sets itself up against the knowledge of God, and we take captive every thought to make it obedient to Christ. (2 Corinthians 10:5)

Do not conform any longer to the pattern of this world, but be transformed by the renewing of your mind. Then you will be able to test and approve what God's will is—his good, pleasing and perfect will. (Romans 12:2)

Since, then, you have been raised with Christ, set your hearts on things above, where Christ is, seated at the right hand of God. Set your minds on things above, not on earthly things. (Colossians 3:1–2)

So then, dear friends, since you are looking forward to this, make every effort to be found spotless, blameless and at peace with him. (2 Peter 3:14)

The Process of Finding My Self-Observer
A message from a client

Several years ago Dr. Silvey talked to me about becoming a "self-observer." He explained to me that what it meant was to simply begin to be aware of and observe my actions. As I started this process I began to notice things I was doing that I didn't want to do. Little by little I saw how I treated people in both words and actions. It was showing me sin in my life.

In the beginning I would see the sin after it was done. For example, there were times I was trying to get a problem resolved on the phone. If things weren't happening in the way I thought they should, I would become frustrated and angry at the customer service person on the other end of the phone. I would vent my anger on her. As my frustration increased my tone of voice would change, and then the anger would escalate so that I would raise my voice and dump all my frustrations out on that poor person. When I hung up, I began to realize how terribly I had treated someone who had no power to fix the problem. I would feel horrible and wish that I could apologize, but it was too late.

In the next step of the process I would still see things afterward, but I began apologizing when I could. One example is when I was rude and condescending to a worker at a fast food restaurant. Ten minutes later as I was standing at church with arms raised, worshiping the Lord, I thought to myself, *What's wrong with this picture?* On my way home from church I went back to that restaurant and apologized to that young man I treated so harshly. I asked the Lord to help me do better the next time I was in that situation.

Little by little I would catch myself before I sinned with my attitude and words. I began to see things from the other person's perspective. Becoming a self-observer has helped me to think of the other person and given me more discernment, kindness, and spiritual maturity over time. Before I speak, I think of how I respond to others and whether my words will help them or hurt them. I can discern if I'm even supposed to say anything to the person or into the situation. I can allow God to be God and let the Holy Spirit do His work in them and pray for them. It has brought my relationship with the Lord closer because I'm dependent on Him to continue to teach me as I walk in relationship with Him and others. If I hadn't learned to be a self-observer, I believe I would still be a pretty immature follower of Christ.

Signed, Grateful for growth and change

Helpful Steps and Perspectives to Opening Our Eyes and Our Ears of Perception

Do you have eyes but fail to see and ears
but fail to hear? (Mark 8:18)

Step #1 Guided and Purposeful Reflection

Start where you are right now in this moment. Often, most people start this process by observing "after the fact" of the incident. As they become familiar with the process, the insight this provides moves them forward and begins to help them anticipate and finally think ahead. A helpful exercise in this process is to ask yourself one of the following questions at the end of each day followed with a second question. After the first question, there is a response from a client.

First Question: Was I sensitive to my feelings without ignoring them or overreacting to them today?

> "I recall a conversation with my mother where she is asking me what time I got up on my day off. 'Did you get up late and waste your day?' she asks. I ask her why it's so important to her to know that information. 'Because I'm your mother, and I'm concerned with how much sleep you need.' I thank her for her concern and tell her I'm doing fine. She asks again, and I say that I've noticed she seems very concerned about how others are doing, and why is that? She stutters a bit and says she's concerned. Again I say I'm doing fine, and this time she lets it go, reluctantly.

"Overreacting for me would have been to buckle and tell her what she wanted to know. I didn't do that this time. Her questions are hurtful, and I was a little angry."

Second Question: Was I in front of the question? (This is a reference to observing after the moment, in the moment, or before the moment.)

"Caller ID is a godsend. Usually my mom calls early to 'help me' get up and get going in the morning. I saw it was her calling before I answered the call. In the past these prying questions leave me shamed that I need more rest than my hyperactive brother. I used to be blindsided by these loaded questions and mourn for days. I felt like I was a bad person. I kept trying to explain myself to her in the hopes that a breakthrough would give me this relationship I crave with Mom.

"One day a new question occurred to me: 'What was wrong with me that I kept knocking at a door that had never opened in all my years of knocking?' I realized she isn't going to change, but I can. All of that to say, today I was in front of the question. I pretty much knew what she was after, something to gossip about. I get angry with that. I've always answered her questions in the past but realize I needn't. I wasn't mean but drew a line and I feel good about how I handled things."

Step #2. The Mirror in Others

A second step is asking other people to be a mirror to help you see yourself more clearly. Choose the people carefully to "reflect back" to you. Their feedback is of little value unless it is open, honest, and accurate. Select someone you trust. Pray specifically, asking God to lead you to someone.

A word of caution to you in the selection process. If you sense certain people feel they have mastered or achieved mastery in their personal life or that this is an area where they feel accomplished, avoid choosing them as your mirror. Instead, be alert for individuals who value growth and are consistent and authentic. Places you might find a growing and developing person might be a support group that you are already involved with such as the Genesis Project. You could consider joining or forming a group for this purpose. Be specific with clarification about how you ask people for this help; here is a sample:

> "I'm in a section of a book that is focusing on self-awareness. It suggests asking someone to act as a mirror in reflecting attitudes, values, and interactive patterns that I have so that I have a better understanding of who I am and can improve my relationships. I'm wondering if we could meet and talk on a regular basis to explore that, and if you're interested, I'd be happy to provide that same mirroring to you as well."

Again, be specific in the type of feedback you want. Here are some examples:

> "My wife says that the kids cry a lot when I'm around. She says I'm too hard on them. I really love them, but she says I give the opposite message. I don't get it; I don't know what she's talking about. Looking at myself is really hard to do, so I guess I'd like to understand what I'm doing or not doing that's giving out this unloving message."

> "I'm thinking it would be helpful for you to give me feedback on picking up subtle clues in conversation and relationship. For some reason, I just don't seem to catch them. I'm trying pretty hard in my conversations with my wife to notice these, and so I'd love your input in that area."

Another individual clarified her mirroring needs this way:

> "My husband absolutely shuts up when I'm around. I try hard to engage him in conversation, but he specializes in one-word answers that drive me crazy. I've felt all these years that he is just totally inept, but since I've been reading this book, I've wondered if I'm doing something, without being aware of it that he is reacting to. Okay, so it feels super vulnerable to say this, but will you help me take a look at that and be a safe person that I can talk to?"

As insightful and trusted as any individuals may be whom you choose to mirror for you, it is important to remember that they will bring their own perspective to the feedback they provide you. This means that what they say will be first drawn through their own development filter. An interesting statistic was developed years ago known as the 80/20 Principle. It indicated that in every interaction 80 percent of a person's perspective is about the self and comes from within. This 80/20 principle will be addressed in depth later in the book, but I included it here so you will be aware that the person you have chosen to give you feedback may be experiencing their own feelings and stresses.

If the feedback that you receive is not helpful, (and undoubtedly there will be those times) remember that you are in a process that will need adjusting. When problems come up, this is an opportunity to clarify what you are really wanting or needing from him or her. Clarify, clarify, and clarify.

Growth Is Worth the Process

"Hey, Javon, how's it going?"

"I'm angry," he says with a scowl.

"What about?"

His reply: "Oh, I don't know."

"I used to say the same thing, Javon, and then I discovered that when I really thought about it, I could always figure out what it is that is really bothering me. I don't always like what I find, but I can process through it." When I talked with Javon, the next day, he told me I was right, and he had figured it out.

This exchange between a client and his friend demonstrates the contagious nature of discovery and growth. As happy as I am to know I have a part in these breakthroughs, I know and you need to know that growth has a cost. You probably already know this, and by the way, ignorance does have a cost as well. But the self has many elaborate protective mechanisms for the ignorant side. You've heard, I'm sure, that "ignorance is bliss," and many believe it.

Seeing the truth of who you really are can be a scary and painful thing indeed, and I agree with Solomon, "With much wisdom comes much sorrow; the more knowledge, the more grief" (Ecclesiastes 1:18).

In the story above, I know what "I don't always like what I find" means. This client was taught that all emotions generally, and his emotions specifically, didn't matter. So when he was angry and discovered that he was upset because he'd had his feelings hurt, an internal judging was going on that went something like this:

> "I'm angry because I have hurt feelings, but my feelings shouldn't matter, should they? Am I that petty that I let a small thing like hurt feelings affect me, and make me angry?"

For him, it was a difficult thing, a sort of huge flaw, a hard-to-acknowledge piece of himself. Of course, he sees this differently now, but it was initially painful to change his view of what he thought he knew to be true.

> "I told my sister she needs to get some counseling. She told me that she wouldn't consider it because she didn't want to end up like me—you know, thinking about everything! Is there some other way to work through your issues?"

The answer is no. You cannot work through anything without thinking about it. People, emotionally and interpersonally, are like a rock that rolls downhill. The place where it comes to rest tends to be the place that it hunkers down in and calls home. In therapeutic terms, they're stuck. That's where many people live their entire lives: stuck. (Actually in therapeutic terms it would probably be more like "they consolidate their sense of self, and it tends to rigidify and be resistant to change.") Rocks do not tend to climb back uphill without the exertion of some external force. Applying the rock analogy, people tend to remain where they are without a good bit of external force impelling them to move up the mountain of God to where He is calling them to be more like Christ. And like those humble rocks, we can expect that having our rough edges knocked off will hurt, sometimes more than a bit, but climbing the hill is our Christian journey. We are to bear fruit, not grow moss.

CHAPTER 3

THE O IN SOCA
Other-Person Perspective

The second step in constructing the new and improved "us" is the *O* in SOCA. It refers to developing the capacity to get inside the perspective of others and really understand their behavioral motivations and words as if looking through their eyes at life. Understanding the position of others is done best when we are able to observe without judging, condemning, and attempting to fix, instead really focusing on listening.

Listening is an immensely important and valuable tool. You will not be able to truly understand another person's perspective without effective listening. For example, it is hard to listen when you are talking, so the acronym WAIT (Why Am I Talking?) is a helpful reminder when in conversation with another person.

Learning to listen well takes practice. Am I giving my full attention to the other person? Am I using eye-to-eye communication with her? Am I absorbing her words and tone, or have I been formulating the response in my mind while she is talking?

Listening with clarifying questions and appropriate nonverbal cues has the added bonus of conveying our love and care, something our world today greatly needs. It is sad to me when the only safe place to be heard is the counselor's office. When did the church stop being a safe place to be heard and be understood?

> In one of our sessions, Ron told me that he is stopping to make sure he understands his wife, Beth, when they are in conversations. He now asks her questions to make sure he gets the message and does not get stuck on the words or her emotional level. He reported that the arguments and distance between them is about 60 percent better. He knows he still needs to develop better listening skills to understand her, but feels like he is making progress.

Some tips when talking with others might include these: Listen without distractions, ask clarifying questions, refrain from giving advice or trying to fix their problems, encourage them toward creating their own solutions, spend less time evaluating and more time trying to understand. Objectivity is just as important here as it is with self-observing.

As we develop other-person perspective, we begin to notice words, actions, and the nonverbal communication skills. We will more often consider the intent and the background. We use questions to help clarify and deepen our understanding of the speaker's point of view. We begin to catch the feelings and the underlying mood between the words.

With experience being an effective Self-Observer we begin to notice when the conversation is hooking into our own issues so that we will not project our feelings and view into the conversation. This takes practice and more practice.

Walk in my shoes for a mile and then you will understand

Other-person perspective is in a sense an extension of self-observation, but instead of developing our capacity to observe ourselves, we expand this to include the "others" that surround our lives. When you have other-person perspective, you are aware of the other person's feelings, thoughts, and point of view. This observation of others is key in activating compassion, empathy, and understanding for the people in your life. If we consider that the basic need of every person is to be heard, understood, and cared for from birth to death, then it follows that understanding, really understanding, is only possible through walking in their shoes, seeing life as it is seen through their eyes. I asked Bev how she developed an effective other-person perspective.

> Working with trauma survivors for the past twenty-five-plus years, I have grown in my ability to read, understand, and form a picture of what the other person is experiencing. Individuals with intense past trauma are experts at hiding their real feelings, avoiding the real meaning, and saying the words they believe you want to hear. I began by watching the body language, facial expressions, and tone of their words, not just what was being said. I remember a statistic that only 20 percent of what we are saying is the meaning; 40 percent is body language, and another 40 percent is tone of voice. So if a client says, "Everything is fine, I am okay," in a scared tone

and in a submissive position, what will I believe the true 20 percent of the meaning is? Not what they are speaking with their words! I usually would say, "You know, *fine* is a four-letter word not be used in the office. Now what is really going on?" Other-person perspective takes practice, with open ears and eyes to observe the real message in the conversation.

How open are your eyes and ears? Just as with self-observation, the observation of others is not to be critical or judgmental but objective and thoughtful.

Not this: These kids are determined to make my life a living hell. Every time I turn around, they are into some awful mischief. What have I done to deserve this? I wish I didn't have to work so hard and leave the kids with my parents all the time. I hate my life!

Better: Wow, why are the kids arguing and fighting so much today? They usually aren't like this, nor do they usually do the opposite of what I'm asking. I wonder why? What is this telling me about them in this moment? Well, we were out very late last night. I wonder if they are overtired. I wonder if things went well when they were with their grandparents yesterday. I need to ask them about anything that might have happened to set this day up to be hard.

In the first example, the question focused not on the children and what clues their behavior could yield, but the parent. The first and reflexive response of many is the tendency toward self-judgment or personal condemnation. Learning to override this jump to judgment in self and others is essential for constructive observation to take place.

Most people generalize their experience onto the lives of others. "I like vanilla ice cream, so you should like vanilla ice cream." "I always wanted to play piano, so you are going to learn to play piano." "I want sex, so ..." Based on a faulty premise, this projection falls short because no two individuals are the same in perspective on life and feelings. Even when we control for factors like environment, there are enormous variations between individuals with very similar backgrounds.

Consider twins. Even identical twins can have very different likes and dislikes, very different approaches to life. If there is this variation between individuals with the same heredity, family status, and environmental factors what about those with circumstances and history vastly differing from your own? Those adept in other-person perspective understand these differences and consider these factors in understanding others.

> One thing I have learned by sitting in the therapist chair is that what spouses perceive is happening is usually not what is happening. A wife says, "Why can't you put the kids to bed for me?" Husband responds with "I'm trying to get this dishwasher fixed so you'll stop complaining!" What the wife hears is "He says I complain and nag all the time!" and what the husbands hears is "She thinks I don't

spend enough time with the kids." Neither the wife nor the husband is trying to see the situation from the other's point of view. Wife is tired and just needs a break, while husband was criticized at work and now is trying to prove he is a good provider, fixer, and dad. Words can be hurtful and when not clarified can lead to years of miscommunication and pain.

Thoughtful observation opens a window of understanding. We are able to see connections between what people say and do with how they are feeling. We can recognize their stress through their posture, attitude, words, and tone of voice. These are just a few of the clues that shed light on how their internal world is managed.

Integrating an understanding of an individual's level of development, without judgment or criticism, is a major milestone forward in other-person perspective skill development. The above couple has since learned to stop and ask a question that is very simple yet opens up the door to communication easily: "What do you need from me right now?" Just a few meaningful words have changed their perspective of their spouse and their marriage. Add these words to your other-person perspective process.

From another client:

"Okay, Murl," the client intoned, "I need your help in learning better communication skills. How can I communicate to my mother how she is hurting me? I've tried and tried, and she just doesn't get it."

I responded, "Didn't you tell me that she doesn't listen to you, can't describe her own feelings, only talks about others? Considering her level of development, she can't. She lacks the capacity to have the conversation you want, but that doesn't stop you from developing caring boundaries with your mother even if she never changes."

Other-person perspective is a powerful tool but not necessarily always used for good. Manipulators are adept at reading people, looking for signs of weakness to exploit. It is vitally important to employ the Christian virtues in the use of this valuable skill. Our goal then is to "Put on love" so that we can "Love our neighbor" (see Colossians 3:14; Matthew19:19).

Other-Person Perspective Questions

1. Do I listen and observe others to understand their intent, not just their words or actions?
2. Do I pay attention to the emotional significance of what the other person is saying or doing?
3. Am I observant of possible intent in others? Am I able to predict (guess or infer) their intent or motivations?
4. Do I ask questions to clarify whether my interpretation of their intent is accurate? Do I check the accuracy of my interpretation through clarifying questions?
5. Do I really listen and pay attention in conversation, or am I distracted, dividing my attention between the other person and something else at the same time?

6. Do I care about this person, as God would desire me to care?
7. Do I notice the nonverbal cues that help me better understand the other person?
8. Do I try to consider factors that may distort understanding, such as age and culture, among others?
9. Do I let my biases override my objectivity in understanding this person?
10. Am I patient to get the whole message spoken, or do I just jump to my own conclusions?
11. Do I observe and listen for more than just the superficial level of the other person's words and actions?
12. Can I have the heart of God toward others when they are hurting me, asking God for the grace to forgive them?

Read me like a book from a client's view:

> I have always been highly attuned to the feelings of others since I was very young. Being aware of the angry feelings of my parents helped me make myself very scarce when it wasn't safe. I internalized their negative feelings. I thought they were angry with me. I brought this childhood distortion right into my adult relationships. As a consequence my relationships have been a disaster.

> I'm always trying to calm my partners' ruffled feathers to appease them and "make them happy." It just doesn't work. I could never seem to "make" them happy, and I was miserable. I was so busy learning about what they wanted and "making" what they

wanted a priority for them; that I never spent any time figuring out what I wanted. I really didn't even know who I was. Although I was highly attuned to negative feelings in others, there was a lot that I missed. I was frequently blindsided by people and events.

Learning about other-person perspective has helped me dial into the clues that people are giving out in conversation all the time. I know now that I can't really make anyone happy. Being happy is a choice that I can't make for others. Letting them be responsible for their own happiness has taken a huge burden off my shoulders. I feel so much more free, and in some ways peaceful like I've never been before in my life.

Developing Other-Person Perspective

Open My Eyes, Lord

If you want to be aware of and helpful to others, not to mention gaining insights to improve your own life and relationships, learn to open your other-person perspective eyes. In order to live life fully, you need to see yourself and others clearly. Do not use rose-colored glasses. Remember that those who are blind cannot lead the blind (Luke 6:39–42). Ask God to help you really see, hear, and understand others.

The Long Haul

The development of other-person perspective takes patience, and it takes time and energy partly because a surprising amount of other-person perspective is about us. Each of us comes to every relationship and conversation with a set of filters that combine to form a grid through which we evaluate what other people say and do. The filtering grid is comprised of our previous experiences that go all the way back to our childhood. As hard as it is to believe, 80 percent of communication originates not in the conversation but in our history; it is more about our grid and us than the actual words exchanged.

At this point it is useful to step back a moment and take a look at the varied layers in a conversation. Our grid picks up the words, and it helps us formulate words for our response, but beneath the others' words and ours lies another message, an emotional message.

> "You are so late that the dinner is ruined. You do this all the time!"

> "But Tina, I don't run out of gas every night, and as I recall, you drove the truck the last time and without filling it when you were done— as I found out the hard way! Don't expect me to be your mother; you can look at the gas gauge!"

And on it goes with guns blazing: the conflict moves toward an all-out war, and when it's all over, both combatants wonder how they ended up here. Jeff's reaction is a defense that escalates. What if instead he had listened to and replied to Tina's unstated message?

> "You are so late that the dinner is ruined. You do this all the time!"

> (Sounds like she's pretty disappointed. Oh, there are candles on the table; she was doing something special

here. I wonder if she was doing something special just for me.) "Whoa! You really went to a lot of work for us, honey. I'm sorry that I wasn't here on time. I can see that dinner meant a lot to you."

"Jeff, did you remember that it's our six-month anniversary?"

(Hmm, she went all out. She wants to know that she is important enough for me to remember these special dates.) "I'm sorry I'm late, but glad that I'm home to be with you. I love you very much!"

Getting to this different place of communicating isn't easy or simple, but it is possible and worth the effort. Isn't it what we all long for in our relationship? The great part about developing other-person perspective skills: it helps you! As you develop a self-observer, you can know whether your internal 80 percent is distorting your awareness of others, and you can learn to listen and respond to underlying messages that bring peace instead of inflaming conflict. But those are just two potential benefits.

Have you ever wondered why you just couldn't connect with someone? It's likely that distortion was creating gaps of understanding, barriers to the deeper level of understanding and intimacy you were hoping for. Growing in your skill to accurately "read" others fills these gaps, giving insight to adjust those filters. It's like cleaning and polishing really dirty, scratched glasses so that you are more able to accurately see the others in your life.

And by the way, those others aren't strangers; they're usually the ones that you love—the ones that you want to understand and support you and who really want support and understanding from you as well. Thus the old saying, "We often hurt the ones we love or who love us the most." Why? Because of one thing: we care about what they say. Think about it, if the grocery store clerk is a jerk, you'd probably say, "What's that guys problem?" but if your husband said the same words to you, it would affect you differently, wouldn't it? Another reason comes from our scratched and dirty glasses. We make judgments based on our inaccurate perceptions.

> "He was hired to clean, but he didn't," one staff member lamented to another. "If we washed his glasses, then maybe he'd see the dirt and clean my classroom."

The truth was perhaps a bit different than this. We rush to wash the glasses of others and "fix them" as quickly and efficiently as possible so that we can get on with things. We often can be too simplistic and not realize that we aren't really able to clean the glasses of others until we have cleaned our own.

Jarrett's Story

> Juneo was born in Japan, and I was born in Portland, Oregon. We met in Japan when I was stationed there with the Navy. We fell in love and eventually married. We came back to Portland to live, and soon afterward things began to change. In Japan, my wife was very submissive and took care of the household things. After we moved to Portland, had children,

and became involved in a church, my wife started to develop her own identity—an identity that was not as submissive as in Japan yet loving and caring toward others. If I had not developed the skill of other-person perspective, we would have not communicated well with each other, would have fought more and likely would have become very intense. I was able to observe and appreciate my wife as the wonderful person she was developing into. I am thankful I spent time in my earlier adult years working on my own self so I might be more committed in our relationship.

Using Jesus' example of removing the splinter from the eye of another (Matthew 7:3–5), we would want that delicate task done very, very carefully! Learn to take your time. We need to approach others with the same care and compassion we would wish for ourselves. So once again, put on love, as you become a student in the classroom of "others." Speeding to interpretations invokes the admonition against "rushing to judgment," and really, our goal isn't to judge at all but to objectively observe with an earnest desire to understand.

Let's imagine that you really did get a splinter in your eye. You go to the doctor, and without hearing a word that you have to say, she grabs for some sharp pokey implements. Then she pins you to the table and yells for you to hold still while she "helps you"—and worst of all, she gets busy on the wrong eye.

That's about the polar opposite of what any of us would wish for from a doctor. We'd want someone who listened carefully to how it got there and how much it hurt. We'd expect her to have lots of questions:

"Which eye is it in? When did it happen? Where in your eye is the splinter?"—for starters. We would expect a careful explanation of what she planned to do to get it out. We'd want her to be calm and objective.

This is actually a pretty good analogy for the potential good and harm that is possible through our interaction in the lives of others. And the good doctor sets out a helpful pattern that can be expanded in a useful way for improving sick relationships. I have included several explanations and suggestions for you to explore and practice.

The first is an interactive model that you can use every day in conversation, followed by the benefits of group work and some journaling prompts. Even though these steps have been listed in a linear fashion, they are much more fluid in real conversation. Your analysis won't necessarily march through each of these four steps, although this order can be very helpful initially as you get started.

The Clarification Cycle:

Starting in the upper left box with during the conversation, the first
step is to identify

    a.   What is their intent?

Moving to the lower left box, next we have to ask ourselves

    b.   What are their words and their nonverbal language?

Then moving to the lower right-hand box, we have to ask

    c.   What am I observing that I heard?

Then moving to the upper right hand-box, we have to ask

    d.   What is my interpretation of what was just said?

Application:

1.   Intent/motivation?

      Begin with a question, bearing two things in mind:

    a.   First, people don't generally state their intent. For example, we don't hear, "The reason that I'm shunning you is because I'm hurt." Like good communication detectives we look for clues: "Bill's been avoiding me lately. I wonder if that conversation about politics offended him. He's been awfully quiet since then."

    b.   Second, their intent could be an emotional message that is entirely different from the verbal message. Imagine a freight train loaded with heavy feelings. The engine is the intent but is being driven intensely by all the feelings, mostly unresolved and unseen. We store up unresolved feelings and often cash them in at unfortunate opportunities.

2.   What do I actually hear? What do I really see?

      What are the words that are spoken? What are the non-verbal clues of the face, posture, attitude and voice intonation?

a. What's the message?

    Conversations are filled with more than words. Sometimes, cryptically, there are underlying messages. In response to the question, "How are you doing?" the answer "Fine" might not actually mean fine. Depending on tone of voice and facial expressions, it could mean exactly the opposite.

b. From an earlier example, our staff member hypothesized that the custodian couldn't see the dirt and that was why he didn't actually clean it up. His behavior revealed a differing message. He could be observed going from room to room, talking with anyone who would listen to him. Seeing the dirt and cleaning clearly wasn't his priority! His message was more like "I have a need to be heard, and I'll clean when I get around to it."

3. Consider the interpretation.

    You've formed a hypothesis; now verify it through the use of thoughtful questions. Are you being reactive or objective? We are prone to interpret other people's words and actions quickly through our feelings, and our response is often a reaction. We emotionally react before we think. It takes conscious effort to recognize this to be objective. Consider your 80 percent. Are the words really saying the message that you heard, or are you hearing the other person without distortion?

4. Clarify, Clarify, Clarify

    Forty years of experience as a psychologist has shown me the power of the right question. A good question is the master key of the mind. It does not come across to others as criticism or as implying that they are a problem (or are causing a problem) but as a desire to know and understand them. Test your hypothesis now through questions: "I'm wondering, did the conversation with your boyfriend go as you'd planned?" "You haven't stopped smiling since you walked in the door. Did he propose?" "That's the third time you slammed that door. Is it not closing properly?" "When I suggested that we split the household jobs, I noticed you became very quiet, I'd like to hear what you are thinking, if you're comfortable sharing."

As you'll note in the diagram at the beginning of this section, clarification is part of an ongoing cycle. Jumping in at any point in the loop opens the conversation toward a greater depth of understanding and might sound something like this:

#1. "Honey, I'm home." (Slams the door, kicks the dog, and drops his bag.) "What's for dinner?"

#2. Hmmm, friendly greeting, usual questions and statements, but what's with the bag, dog, and door? He seems irritated about something. Wasn't this way when he left this morning. I wonder if it's his review. He was supposed to be getting that back today.

#3. I wonder if he got a bad review. He's been worried that might make staying with the company shaky.

#3. Bad review seems plausible. I know he worries about his job.

#1. "We're having your favorite, hamburger gravy with extra lard over biscuits. Say, did you have your review today? I know that you've been thinking a lot about that lately. I was wondering how it went."

#1. "Actually, I did have the review today, and it went great! It kind of shocked me. You know, I've been worrying about my job. They're a hard bunch to read, but the review was stellar, and the boss couldn't be happier."

#2   Now that I'm looking at him, he seems upbeat and happy. It sure wasn't the job that's got him upset.

#3. I think that's a bit of a stretch. I'm kind of stumped!

#1. "Honey, are you upset about something?"

#1. "No, why do you ask?"

#2. "Well, you slammed the back door, and the dog yelped, and you didn't set your bag down, you dropped it. I just thought you might be upset about something."

#1. "When I walked in the back door, my arms were full. I actually tripped over the dog, couldn't see her. That wasn't my bag, that was me hitting the floor, and I guess I was ticked at the dog and did slam the door after I put her out, but I'm not really all that upset now. Say, can we figure out a way to keep her from sleeping right in front of the door?"

#2. Hmmm, I'm wondering if that lard gravy comment is a hint. Is she irritated with cooking tonight?

#3. We'd planned to go out sometime this week I wonder if she's hoping it's going to be tonight.

#3. That sounds plausible. It's 7:00, and we usually eat before now.

#1.   "What would you think about saving the biscuits and gravy for some other night and going out for dinner?"

Journaling Opportunities

Another tool to use in developing other-person perspective is taking time to reflect at the end of each day. Take time to note the new insights that you are gaining about the "others" in your life. What is surprising to you, perhaps a bit scary with this new way of relating to others?

Journaling can be especially helpful following difficult conversations. Here are some helpful questions to consider as you reflect and write.

"Was there any communication during the day that led to confusion or misunderstanding between us?"

"Was a solution reached in the situation?"

"Do I understand the other-person's perspective more clearly, or am I more confused?"

"What parts of the conversation would I like to revisit for clarification?"

"What are some questions that could reveal more of her perspective?"

"Are there parts of his perspective that I could more fully understand"?

Another opportunity to practice this skill, with or without the journaling, is to read between the lines in the Bible. As you are reading, take time to see through the perspective of the writer. Create a mental image of that moment in history (what was life like at the time it was written?), and weave in the culture and feelings of this man or woman. As you are imagining the biblical character's life, ask how proficient this person was at being self-observing and whether he or she had developed other-person perspective.

Small Group

Being part of a small group can be very beneficial in the development of self-observer and other-person perspective. Activities to consider in this context would be role-plays where two members spin a scenario, and the rest of the group becomes the audience who hypothesize what the messages are behind the words and other verbal and nonverbal communication.

Another possibility, after establishing the ground rule "What's shared in the group, stays in the group" and participants feel that it's safe to share, is discussing personal puzzling experiences from their lives. The group can pose and explore possible meanings and clarification questions.

Finally, participants can act as mirrors for each other. This calls for another ground rule: What is shared isn't judged. Instead, it is reflected back, and if the reflector is unclear, then clarifying questions can help the person sharing practice exploring and articulating feelings and creating hypotheses for his or her personal puzzles.

CHAPTER 4

THE C IN SOCA
Consequential Thinking

O be careful, little eyes, what you see.
O be careful, little eyes, what you see.
There's a Father up above
And He's looking down in love,
So be careful, little eyes, what you see.

O be careful, little ears, what you hear.
O be careful, little ears, what you hear.
There's a Father up above
And He's looking down in love,
So, be careful little ears what you hear

O be careful, little hands, what you do.
O be careful, little hands, what you do.
There's a Father up above,
And He's looking down in love,
So be careful, little hands, what you do

O be careful, little feet, where you go,
O be careful, little feet, where you go,
There's a Father up above
And He's looking down in love,
So be careful, little feet, where you go.

O be careful, little mouth, what you say.
O be careful, little mouth, what you say.
There's a Father up above,
And He's looking down in love,
So be careful, little mouth, what you say.

Remember this Sunday school song from childhood? We would stand up, clapping and singing loudly those memorized words, not realizing the importance of their meaning or the consequences of what would happen when we did not watch our eyes, ears, hands, feet, or mouth.

From a client:

> Being raised in a stricter church environment as a
> child, I was scared when we would sing this song
> and often would stubbornly not sing the fifth verse.
> "Be careful, little mouth, what you say" ... well, I
> wasn't too careful because I was often, more often
> than not, in trouble for my mouth. I was an expert at
> back-talking to my parents, only my parents. I surely
> would not do that to anyone else.
>
> As I became a teenager, this became a proverbial
> problem, one from which I receive many, many
> consequences—severe consequences, I thought at
> the time. And I did not like any of them. As a young
> mother with children of my own I began to realize
> the importance of consequences for our behavior
> or sometimes consequences because of the lack of
> certain behaviors.

The third step to consider on the pathway to Christian maturity
in SOCA is *C*—consequential thinking. If we consider these song
verses—better yet, if we applied these song verses and followed
them—how much pain and grief we could avoid. So could the world,
and your church and my church. Being careful, putting thought
behind if not ahead of our feet, our words, and our impulses is what
consequential thinking is all about. It's thinking ahead to what might
happen if I say this angry word, if I buy this beer, if I drive eighty
miles an hour, or if I sneak to that porn site. No one will know, we
tell ourselves—but they will!

Consequential Thinking

This is the ability to predict and anticipate with accuracy the potential outcomes or results of a given course of action. Consequential thinking is the ability to see cause and effect not in the rearview mirror but in the mind's awareness process. It's nothing more or less than thinking ahead to potential results, effects, and ramifications. What is going to happen if I drove down this road at eighty MPH? Think ahead, either through past experiences or common sense. We all have the ability to think ahead, but many of us are impulsive and react immediately.

> At my grandpa's farm my dad had a big pile of used lumber. He told us kids to be very careful of stepping on the boards because they were filled with nails. Now in my five-year-old brain I thought, "I'm wearing shoes. Nails can't go through shoes." So I looked for a long nail and purposely stepped on it to see what would happen. I found out and gave out a wild wail! To this day my dad doesn't know that I did it on purpose; he still blames himself for leaving nails poking up.

From Murl:

> My father was quite the blacksmith. Dad would let me watch while he heated metal white hot, and then he would twist, hammer, and shape it. I loved it! "Be careful not to touch this" was his warning, but I was so curious to see what would happen that I did it

anyway. I'll never forget the smell of burning flesh. Even after seventy years, you can still see the scar on my finger.

These stories beautifully illustrate what the lack of consequential thinking leads toward: pain and problems. Ignorance is not bliss. The discovery, at the point of a nail and the sizzle of skin, that actions have consequences. These normal childhood experiences make mental connections that help guide our adult lives. Experiences shape our ability to accurately predict what the result of a particular direction may be. But what if these little boys hadn't learned? What if they were never allowed to experience the consequences of bad choices as a child? We need look no farther than our burgeoning prison population to see where people might end up. Consider how so many encumber their lives with staggering debt or ruin their marriages through moments of impropriety.

My favorite Darwin Award story is about one man who strapped a booster rocket to the roof of his car and lit it. From the skid marks on the pavement it was clear in the first quarter mile that he was aggressively applying his brakes (apparently he was having second thoughts). The skid marks ceased when the car became airborne. His ride ended abruptly against the distant canyon wall. Fortunately, most mistakes don't end with this kind of finality, and if you have just begun working on developing consequential thinking foresight, know that you really can change your patterns and learn to predict unwanted outcomes. Learning to avoid them may take a bit longer. Ours is not the first generation that has struggled with thinking things through before starting.

This is such an important skill that God weighed in with some sage advice to help us develop. Being able to consider future potential benefits or problems of an action is a major component in wisdom, and blindly and rashly going forward without a plan or passing though is part of the definition of *foolishness*. The Bible has a lot to say about this, with over eighty scripture verses on *wisdom* and more than two hundred on *fool, fools, foolish,* and *foolishness*. The natural consequence of wise planning, *rewards*, is mentioned eighty times. Knowing and predicting basic consequences and steering clear of trouble is the entry level of wisdom. It defines circumspection that spells success on earth, but there is something even more important that is beyond this world.

What we have faith in has enormous consequences for our present and the life to come. "What good is it for a man to gain the whole world"—every advantage and every possession that the world has to offer—"and yet lose or forfeit his very self?" (Luke 9:25). If we consider the things of this life and believe that the decisions we make are good, without seeking the leading of the Spirit, there are consequences both now and for eternity.

In Randy Alcorn's book, *Heaven*, he asked a simple question, "In light of eternity, what choices or decisions have you made for the Lord today?" I love those words that encourage me to ponder the choices I have made. It is almost as if every choice has some profound consequence here on earth and beyond. Oh, wait a minute; our choices do have consequences, both earthly and eternal.

Consequential thinking considers the result of an action. It considers whether the reasoning used to predict an outcome is correct.

Thinking ahead looks at our own history. For example, enjoying one drink and good conversation sounds okay unless the reality of my history of alcoholism makes only one drink extremely unlikely. And finally remember the input of the wise and the wisdom of God. "How much better to get wisdom than gold, to choose understanding rather than silver!" (Proverbs 16:16).

Consequential Thinking Questions

1. Do I consider the benefits or problems of a potential action, including what I say and how I say it?
2. Do I evaluate my words or actions based on past experiences for benefit or for potential problems?
3. Do I consider the circumstances, people, or culture involved in the present choice?
4. Do I use God's Word to help me consider the consequences?
5. Do I let my biases or emotions cloud my ability to evaluate my actions or words?
6. Do I just do or say things and not consider the consequences?
7. Do I let the fear of potential consequences keep me stuck in the familiar?
8. Do I look ahead, or do I let things build up and then just reap the consequences?
9. Do I go so fast that I am always looking at the consequences after they have already happened?
10. Do I consider consequences for myself for the future or just in the present moment?
11. Did I consider the leading of the Spirit in my choice?

Developing Consequential Thinking

"It will take me farther than I want to go, keep me longer than I want to stay and cost me more than I want to pay."

Consequential thinking begins even before the self-observer and other-person perspective concepts are fully developed. You see it in young children as they are figuring out how the world works. "I said please before I took it. So Mommy, why is he so angry" "I said I was sorry, but he's still angry, and he shouldn't be if I said I'm sorry." For young children their relational understanding is black and white. Their way of viewing how relationships work is almost a magical way of thinking. Progressing to greater levels of understanding is coupled with the development of self-observer and other-person perspective. In conjunction with these other tools, we are able to understand the true consequences at a deeper level.

> Mommy: "Tommy, when you took his teddy bear, he was very sad. I know that you said please, but please is asking only; it was not permission to take. See him sitting in the corner and crying? He is doing that because he misses his teddy bear and because you took it without him saying that you could."

> Tommy: "I sorry, Mommy, I sorry he sad. I give him Teddy back."

In this example, our little teddy taker's mother tries to reason with him and create a picture of other-person perspective—his brother crying in the corner over the teddy. Does the little guy understand?

Probably not completely, yet he is beginning to understand that "what I do can make someone sad." Over time as he grows and matures he will begin to realize taking responsibility for his actions is part of consequences.

Responsibility is another major piece of maturing and growing toward understanding others: owning the results of our actions in a way that will inform future actions, creating empathy for those we hurt so that in a way we experience their loss as a sort of psychic pain, an internal deterrent against future poor choices. Learning to walk is best done when you are nearer the ground. The older and taller you are, the farther you fall. For those who weren't able to learn their lessons so young, there are other opportunities to experience this psychic and physical pain, but the costs are now higher, and the consequences cut a wider, more damaging swath: broken relationships, estranged families, costly medical bills or court proceedings, and sometimes death.

The Problem with Seeing inside Myself Clearly

Many will read this and say, "I understand consequential thinking," when actually the understanding is only partial. Some who are adept at predicting outcomes and helpful to others in doing so can be entirely blind when it comes to themselves. Thus, it is actually quite common to not be able to objectively view our own actions and predict outcomes. This inability or blind spot, in part, has a developmental explanation. The growth/learning process almost always starts from the outside in. We learn, observe, and then internalize. As this skill matures, you will find your internal eyes will be sharpened, and you can access this view more easily and with less distortion.

Tom knows he only has two more days to decide if he's going to renew his contract, or go looking for another job. He's had the annual evaluation form for over a month now and just can't decide what to do. There's so much riding on his guaranteed paycheck, but he's always wanted to have a career in a completely different field. He's a nervous wreck!

***

Tina was wondering if Jim would ever propose to her. She really wanted him to, but now that he has, she doesn't know what to do! She thinks she loves him, but now she's not sure what she thinks, because there are so many feelings, and they are coming all at once. She said that she'd tell what she decided in two weeks. If she follows that self-imposed time line, she needs to tell him tomorrow. She's a nervous wreck!

The problem with important decisions is that the greater the significance, the greater the potential for emotionally based distortion. The voices from our past that are shouting in our heads, our historical hooks, our anxiety, and the resulting paralysis can often be circumvented through imagining a detached rather than a personal point of view. Imagine that you are telling a close friend in a similar situation what she might do to reach resolution or reach a decision:

Instead of: "What am I going to do?"
Alternative: "If I were telling someone in my position what to do, what would I tell him?" "If I knew someone

in a similar situation, what words of encouragement would I give her?"

An extension that can be very helpful is to write down the encouragement that you would give this other person and read it out loud to yourself. Or write a letter to yourself from a valued and respected family member or co-worker. Some of my clients journal extensively as a way to sort through thoughts and feelings. Writing is often a good way to slow down the racing mind and bring it back into focus. Writing provides a record of your thoughts, when you are thinking clearly. Journaling can become a source of stability to refer back to in times of confusion or anxiety. For some, journaling brings calm to their thoughts.

Reacting versus Choosing

Bev relates this story:

> I am going to tell on myself! This situation happened many years ago, yet haunts me today. I have asked Murl, "Please don't ask about financial matters late at night, I mean after 9:00 p.m., such as what's in the checking account or how much you spent on whatever."

> On this particular occasion, we both had been at the office for a long day of appointments with clients, it was late, and we were both hungry. He forgot the "don't ask late at night" rule and asked about finances, and I lost it, I mean lost it. I was driving

and immediately floored the pedal, recklessly driving around the curves. Then I abruptly stopped the car in the middle of the road, tore off the sun visor above my seat, and hit him with it. By now I am sure you are laughing out loud as visual images run through your mind. I am less than five feet tall, and Murl is over six feet. Tearing off the sun visor actually was not hard at all—quite easy, in fact! We were in the middle of the road. I can't even begin to type out the string of words that came from my mouth.

I got out of the car and began to walk home. Murl, quite stunned, got in the driver's seat and managed to coax me back into the car, and we proceeded home. I still drive the same car, and to this day can see where the visor is super glued back in its proper place. Now can I analyze this and tell you exactly what happened? Maybe. I do know my emotions were unmanaged, and certainly I did not think about my actions. I just reacted!

Did I give any thought to my actions or just react? Was I choosing or reacting? What do you think? Taking time to ponder is not popular in the heat of the moment, but considering the potential consequence of an action is essential. Otherwise we react by impulses. In addition to impulses, the brain stores patterns of learned behavior. For example, when learning to drive most of us were told to use the 10:00 and 2:00 position when holding on to the steering wheel. Most of us give little active thought after we sit down behind the wheel, and our behavior there is now automatic. Without focused awareness, historical patterns are very resistant to change.

Choice and the ability to choose are aided by considering potential outcomes, and I'm not talking about those who wake up next to a stranger on random mornings or act out addictive behaviors. I'm talking about those destructive vices our culture applauds such as workaholics, obsession with fitness, gossip that is neatly disguised as "praying for," compulsive actions, or any other activity that is done at the cost of relationship. Many today are abundantly rich in things and dirt-poor toward God and the people they love.

Consequential thinking puts the things of valid importance above what life presents for us to focus on at the time.

> Tracy, a very active person who was always doing things for other people and involved in volunteer groups in the community, had not learned to think ahead for herself. Her husband and she were involved with couples; they often would go to local casinos to gamble. Tracy used their credit cards to buy things as well as to pay for the gambling. It did not take long before their credit cards were maxed out with especially high interest. It was at this time that Tracy discovered she was pregnant. Surprised and unprepared, they both realized that they had not made future preparations for a family. She came in for counseling to build better skills of time and money management. She and her husband quickly realized they had not learned consequential thinking skills during their childhood, teens, or early adult years. They worked diligently to develop new patterns in their lives with regard to finances, family values, and future planning.

Consider Forgiveness

Consequential thinking has some unexpected applications. Consider the act of forgiveness, for example. When someone hurts you, you face an important choice, an important opportunity. Holding on to hurts and anger can build up inside to such an extent that this bottling up causes more damage than the original hurt. Forgiveness, on the other hand, is a choice that leads to greater peace.

Many individuals don't forgive because they mistakenly think of forgiveness as a magic wand that takes the relationship right back to where it was before the infraction. They feel they are required to turn the other cheek and just as blindly to allow the other person right back as if nothing ever happened. This is not an accurate understanding of forgiveness. If you forgive someone you still have the choice of how to relate to him or her. You may fully forgive someone and not trust him or her one bit. You may fully forgive someone and not allow him or her back into your home. There is nothing blind about forgiveness, in Christ; God doesn't pretend that we have done nothing wrong. He is clear about the damaging effects of bad choices. His love and forgiveness include choices, and it's okay if ours do as well.

One last aspect of forgiveness is the misconception that it applies only to others. Many carry great burdens of guilt and shame because they feel they cannot forgive themselves. If the all-knowing God of the universe has forgiven you and said there is now therefore no condemnation for those in Christ Jesus, then we have no basis for holding out on ourselves (see Romans 8:1). I encourage you to receive God's love, acceptance, value, and compassion towards you. Receive

God's perspective, forgive yourself, and look with compassion at yourself in your areas of shortcomings.

For some, self-forgiveness is essential before they are able to fully forgive others, while other individuals can easily forgive others but never themselves. Individual attitudes vary, but understanding your own barriers to self-forgiveness and self-compassion is necessary to release your unnecessary burdens of guilt and shame. May you commit to asking God to bless you as you forgive yourself. Ask God for His help, and receive His forgiveness and blessings fully.

Be Anxious for Nothing!

The development of consequential thinking is focused on a future perspective, which may provoke feelings of anxiety for some individuals. All this attention to the countless things that can go wrong as the result of an action can hijack this useful mental exercise and instead result in arousing unreasonable fears for the future. The anxiety unreasonably magnifies potential problems. Take time to calm yourself before proceeding if you feel stirred up. Go for a walk; take a cup of tea outside, and enjoy the sun. Now breathe and journal a page or two; then proceed.

The goal is objectivity. When anxiety is high, the balance of hope is lost, and the future consequences can seem like a mountain of disasters. Our self-observer can alert us to this anxiety, so that we can maintain a helpful perspective in this process. This points out why the development of a healthy self-observer is crucial to consequential thinking and how each element of SOCA is essential and interconnected to the other.

Not Eliminating All Problems but Making Wise Choices

One action may often have consequences both beneficial and problematic. Often our focus is only on identifying and avoiding actions that may have problems associated with them. The flaw with this approach is that many good activities have the potential for major problems.

Take marriage. With the current divorce rate at 60 percent, even among Christian marriages, it is very easy to think of the many potential problems and struggles. However, the opportunity for a growing, caring, and compassionate relationship far outweighs the struggles, making the choice of marriage worth pursuing. Choosing a certain life path may have very difficult problems associated with it but still may be the desired choice because of the good things that are gained. I would have to say sitting in the therapist's chair for all those years was not without its problems; but the gains in relational understanding and the hope in the growth of clients made those problems seem minor in comparison. Our goal is not to eliminate all problems from our lives but to learn to create a way internally to sift through the possible scenarios and then to choose the best option.

When safety equipment is ignored, when we don't ask simple questions such as "Is this broken ladder strong enough to hold me," the results are predictable, and learning how to predict is possible and desirable. A prank at work and the prankster is fired, a wife and child are lost because of an affair—so much brokenness can befall us when wisdom is set aside. Wisdom lifts its voice in the streets and calls out to all who will listen: "Think before you do. Consider carefully the consequences."

There Is Hope for Pain

There is more to consequential thinking than avoiding pain or trouble! At its essence, consequential thinking is learning to exercise insight and employ wisdom as we look into the future. For followers of Christ, it is important to bear in mind that our earthly journey is only part of our story. The rest is best viewed from God's perspective, through the eyes of faith in His promises.

You may have entirely mastered the skill of consequential thinking but still have problems that are not of your own making, and no amount of prayer and foresight could have prevented them or will remove them from your life. It is at this point that many Christ followers become disillusioned, because they are given the false sense that if they love God enough, pray hard enough, and read their Bible enough, all problems are surmountable. No wonder they believe this way, considering how much confusion there is on the subjects of wealth and poverty, sickness and healing. If this describes you, you are certainly in good company, and not just with your contemporaries either. Job had very real questions about suffering, and so did the apostle Paul. Do you remember Paul's thorn in the flesh? He prayed earnestly three times; he wanted it gone and was confident that it would leave. What he learned is that his thorn was a part of his story, not just a barrier to what his life "should" be.

Many who read this are overwhelmed with their own pain and loss in life. Some have genetically caused illness, unwanted sexual tendencies, addictive compulsions, relational conflicts that arise from messed-up childhoods—not to mention the consequences of just old-fashioned mistakes. What do we do when we ask, and pain is not removed or problems resolved? The question arises: Where is God? Does He know that I'm suffering, and does He care?

When Jesus was sweating great drops of blood the night before His execution, He asked if it was possible to cancel the next day's events. God did not do what He asked. Was God with Jesus in that moment? Was He aware of how awful the suffering of His Son was going to be? Did He care?

God is not carelessly tending the earth like some forgetful gardener who skips a watering or feeding here and there and with an "Oops, too bad about that one; wish I gotten back a bit sooner." He is all the beautiful picture that Jesus painted for us: the Good Shepherd who lays his life down for the sheep; the master gardener who carefully tends his vines and fruit trees; the father of the prodigal son, faithful and quick to love, even when we leave him. He is scanning the horizon, longing for our return. We are never forgotten and never alone in our pain. God is our loving Father.

The Father subjected Christ to a short life and the cross, and why? Because this suffering is based on an unrelenting hope that the trial will accomplish a greater good, so that the suffering is a counted cost that left God saying, "It is worth it," and not a grim-jawed "I've counted the cost and crunched the numbers." No! Jesus set His mind joyfully to the cross, joyfully because of you.

God's presence is our light in the darkness of suffering, His rainbow above our lives a promise of hope for meaning and redemption. The promise that our smoldering ashes will be changed out for beauty is an assurance of good that is possible, that is coming, that cannot be stopped—an inevitability for those held in the family hands of God.

Consequential Thinking Activities

1. The greatest consequence we experience is the distance we create between God and ourselves. Consider the saying, "If God seems far away, who moved?" I assure you it was not God. Read the book of Jeremiah, and list all the consequences suffered for turning away from God.

2. Consider your relationships. What are some of the growing and difficult aspects? What are the activities you do in these relationships, and which ones do you avoid? Why do you think this is?

3. One of the most important ways to study consequential thinking is to read the Bible. Study Exodus, Judges, First and Second Samuel, and First and Second Kings, paying attention to the benefits and consequences of each biblical character's actions. As you study these passages, ask yourself, "What would I do in this situation?"

4. Focusing on a Bible character, now go through the consequential thinking questions, and reflect on his or her relative development.

5. Pick a specific time and set an appointment with yourself to reflect on the consequential thinking questions. Write out your answers. Better yet, invite someone you trust to share this appointment with you. Have him complete his own reflection, and then spend time afterward sharing your insights.

6. A good way to help consequential thinking is to choose a week where you will plan and reflect daily. At the end of each day, reflect on the day's plan. What were some of the unexpected consequences? Were they beneficial or harmful? What surprised you today, and why? As you plan for the next day, consider what you expect the effects will be for each element. At the end of the week, summarize what you've learned.

7. Keep a journal. List a new consequence you learned each day. Remember, one action may often have consequences both beneficial and problematic. As you are listing, be sure to list them both, not just the problems that emerge. Choosing a certain life path may have very difficult problems associated with it yet still be the desired choice because of the good things that are to be gained. Our goal is not to eliminate all problems from our lives but to learn to create a way internally to sift through the possible scenarios and then to choose our best option.

8. The biblical use of the word *consider* is just one way God encourages the thoughtful introspection embodied in the concept of consequential thinking. So often we don't consider things; we just do them. When you are able to see things clearly, your internal life is illuminated as to intent and motivations. You are better able to view situations, relationships, and especially yourself with insight, understanding, and compassion (Luke 11:34). What is an area of your life that you wish to consider so you may illuminate your internal growth?

CHAPTER 5

THE A IN SOCA
Alternative Thinking

The fourth and final step in constructing the new and improved "me" is alternative thinking. An alternative perspective is the antithesis of boxed-in thinking, boxed-in living, and a boxed-in relationship with God. Alternative thinking opens rather than narrows our options.

A client's point of view:

> In my family we had rules for everything, and questioning the rules wasn't a good idea because my mom and dad were always right. "Because I said so" ended every appeal, backed by force. Our church denomination was the same: they had the right answer for everything; our hermeneutics and exegesis were just right.

> I knew God. He was like my parents, but instead of "because I said so," He said, "thus sayeth the Lord," which meant the same thing. It was neat and tidy, my life and thinking all laid out in little boxes for me. We had a box for children to live where we were "seen but

not heard," and we had a bigger box for parents, who got to do whatever they wanted. Church was a great big box for us to live in with God, wrapped in shiny gold paper and a big red bow.

I didn't really feel loved by my parents, and love didn't fit to well in our denomination's box either. They had a box for love right next to the wrapped one; we got to visit occasionally when we earned it, which wasn't often because we were never quite good enough. They had plenty of room for sin, though, and large doses of shame, guilt, and condemnation.

So what happens if we try to fit God into our little box? What happens in life when our perspective is closed, narrow, and with only one possible way to choose? How are we limiting ourselves?

Alternative Thinking

Alternative thinking is sometimes called brainstorming, listing as many ideas as possible to broaden options in problem solving. Individuals who can develop the skills in alternative thinking widen their perspective in life and can be creative and original in their ideas. Think of life as a blank canvas, and we get to make decisions about how to make our life beautiful.

Years ago, while in graduate school, I was called in to help a local company do some brainstorming. We were off to a good start, but I found that participants were starting to reject ideas, even as the idea was spoken. I informed them that in the formative process of making the list, there would be no judgment of ideas. All ideas were plausible. Narrowing down the ideas would come later. It was a long and interesting list, and then came the narrowing down. Throw out this idea because it won't work in this setting; this one's too expensive; and on it went until they came to one idea in particular. With some tinkering it became their best-selling product. Here's the funny part? This idea would never have made it to the consideration part of the process, without me jumping in with the reminder of the ground rules judging ideas not too early but later. They weren't even going to write it down. It was then that I realized how important it is to be objective with alternatives and not immediately evaluating them. In the next year, this idea became a huge moneymaker for the company.

Many people live daily in lives stuck in patterns, old patterns that are long overdue for change, patterns that seem stuck, boring, and uncreative.

A client once told me, "It takes great effort for me to try new things. I've driven the same old route, eaten the same old food, lived in the same old house filled with worn furniture, watched the same old shows and then bought the whole season on DVD and watched them again. I do the same workout routine, and for exercise I always ride the same path on my old bike. I've never really thought of doing something different, because it sort of works for me … well, until now. Darn these relationships where different isn't bad. I think it's bad. Why can't she just do things my way? Why do I have to look at options where I like things the way they are?"

And this from Bev:

> When Murl and I married some fifty-one years ago,
> I was determined to keep him in the surprised mode
> most of the time. So I decided to do something different
> every week. Being in school, without excessive
> funds, I found I had to be creative and unique in
> finding ways to be different. Once I decided our small
> apartment close to the university was boring, so I set
> about moving furniture. By the end of day the dining
> room was in the spare bedroom and the office where
> the dining room had been only a few short hours
> before. The living room was rearranged, and when
> Murl came home from a late-night class, he tripped
> over the newly placed couch. I do believe this was the
> beginning of my finding alternative choices to life
> itself. And yes, I still am trying each week to plan
> something that will surprise him—maybe not moving
> the whole house full of furniture around, but having
> dinner in a different place or driving home from the
> office a totally different route. Keeps him guessing!

I have learned that one choice may not work in a given situation, while another choice will not only work but also benefit everyone. Maybe it's driving just one block over and discovering a new "best" antique store or choosing a new cuisine that might light up the palate. There is a reason that God created men and women differently. Actually these differences aren't a threat; they can be complementary, if we recognize and allow alternative choices into our lives.

Karen wrote me this note from her journal:

> So it runs deeper than just the same old day, at the same old job. I'm disappointed with my life, and as much as I resist change at first, I really like it. Then my husband and I had squabbles, and I went back to what was comfortable. As I'm exploring it now, I think it's good that things weren't working because it's made me take a closer look at not just what I do but why I do it.
>
> I have really pretty much one way of seeing myself, which is bad. I feel like I'll never be good enough. It kind of goes all the way back to how my mom treated me. She was busy ignoring me or setting the bar higher for my next task, not really much recognition for what I could do, and since she and God seemed to be on such good terms, well, I figured He must be the same. I'm learning otherwise. Now I'm no longer under the law but grace and have a newfound freedom in Christ.

Realize that you can do things differently and not be wrong (or necessarily right for that matter) and that there are many helpful perspectives on most issues. Just because you've always done it this way, doesn't mean that you must continue to do it this way. This can be a wonderful relief and can bring a new view to life. On specific problems, it can throw off some of the unnecessary constraints that narrow options and instead open up all sorts of new possibilities. To take advantage of this expanded array of choices requires openness. Just how open are you? Are you willing to risk becoming free?

Simply writing a list of possibilities can bring to light all kinds of options and opportunities. You can also visualize alternative thinking as pulling out a map and looking at all of the different ways to reach your destination and then, by the process of elimination, finding the best pathway for the circumstance. Continuing with our trip metaphor illustrates what I mean by "best for the circumstance." Traveling for speed, because "I'm late for a meeting," would probably mean taking a different route than having no time constraints and journeying for pleasure to see the scenery.

SOCA elements build upon and are interdependent on each other. So remember that alternative thinking is important to connect to consequential thinking after the list is made.

As with the other principles of SOCA, what does God have to say about options in problem solving? For starters, He's the God of all creativity. Look at His creation, and ponder just how many ways He's solved the problem of movement in creatures. If it were up to me, I doubt that I would have come up with the kangaroo, and yet there it is on spring-loaded legs and feet, with top speeds of forty mph.

His revelation in the Bible is also very diverse. In His dealings with people it's a bit challenging to see how seldom He's done exactly the same thing twice. For example, the parting of the Red Sea happened only once. In fact, the Old and New Testaments are filled with one-of-a-kind, brilliant shows of creativity. Take Gideon's routing of the Midianites, God told him to reduce his army of thousands till he was down to three hundred. He said: "Arm each man with a water pot, a ram's horn trumpet, and a torch—oh, and attack at night." What the text doesn't say is that that the military strategy of the day typically gave the trumpet and torch to a leader of a contingent of troops. The Midianite mind would multiply the three hundred torches they saw by the typical number of men in a contingent. This illusion distorted the true size of the fighting force to something far larger and more menacing. The psychological effect of this ruse probably explains the panic and routing of Midian. A brilliant military maneuver; God is ingenious!

And oh, yes, He has lots to say about how we live our lives and great advice on which of the many paths available are the best to take. Judges 18:14 (NASB), for example, says, "Now therefore, consider what you should do." Consideration, pondering, and careful thought are essential aspects of alternative thinking and consequential thinking. Let's take a moment now to follow a thread of alternative and consequential thinking through some Bible passages to see where it takes us.

The best alternative may vary according to a diverse array of factors. (Remember, the reason for the trip sometimes determines which route is taken.) What never varies, and is always the best alternative for all people, is to "Now fear the Lord and serve Him with all faithfulness." (Joshua 24:14) "reject the wrong, choose the right" (Isaiah 7:15). Even when evil may look pretty appealing, "pleasing to the eye" (Genesis 3:6), we know its end is death. Also we read "In the way of righteousness there is life" (Proverbs 12:28). The consequence of right choices is that we walk the path of serving, because this path goes right through the gate that opens into eternal life.

Alternative Thinking Questions

1. Am I objective in looking at my alternatives, or do I become rigid, single-minded, easily locked into my preferred option, the way I usually do or view things, the people I associate with, or my customary situational response? In other words, am I open to looking at alternatives, or do I gravitate quickly to my usual response?

2. Do I let past successes or failures disqualify certain viable alternatives, or am I able to look into the past with objective observations?

3. Am I anxious or insecure, so that I don't believe I can come up with a good alternative? (Anxiety and insecurity can block the free flow of ideas.)

4. Do I get stuck in my choice rather than accepting the best choice for all involved?

5. Do I stop and get stuck on the first alternative, without considering those that follow?

6. Do I keep looking at alternatives and find myself unable to make any choice? (If your answer to this one is yes, bear in mind that there are no perfect choices, our goal is to pick the best option in front of us with the information that we have at that moment.)

7. Is looking at alternatives so overwhelming that I just give up completely?

8. Do I wait so long to consider alternatives that I just take the first one that might be an easier or more available alternative?

9. Do I let my emotions—anger, fear, depression—cloud my alternative thinking?

10. Do I use God's word to help me develop alternatives?

11. Do I allow the Spirit to help me with creative alternatives?

Taking Steps to Develop Alternative Thinking

Start Simple, Have Fun

When Bev and I were youth coordinators at the Merced First Baptist Church in Merced, California, we were traveling with the youth to a weekend retreat at the coast. Although most of the young people had been on retreats with us before, many had not. We gathered in the sanctuary and asked the group to think about the rules they wanted for the weekend.

Wow, did they ever come up with some interesting rules: "Don't step on a jellyfish!" "Don't swim out so far you drown!" "Don't eat beans if you fart a lot!" "Don't be so loud that others can't sleep!" And on and on it went! The group had fun yet covered the important bases of safety and courtesy, while making youth involvement entirely inviting. The resulting list is one that Bev and I would never have come up with for them, and it was so much fun that the list of rules was a source of laughter all weekend. It was an activity that set a wonderful tone for the entire retreat.

Now it's your turn. Start with something simple, and write a list as long as possible of alternatives. For example, what can I do today if it rains? Be creative, have some fun, and put in at least a couple of really far-out ideas. Before you start, follow these two guidelines to help you keep an open mind.

1. Don't judge entries initially. Remember, alternative thinking does not evaluate the alternative at the time of its initial listing. The listing step is all about getting as many ideas on paper as possible, so focus on listing, not judging the list.

2. Don't dismiss ideas hastily. Some ideas might be good for a particular season of life but not for another, a good fit for one individual but not good for a group. Because of these great variations it is all the more important to get as many alternatives on the table as possible, without dismissing any.

Now Step It Up

Let's step it up now. Consider a more serious subject, such as money. For many people, how money comes and goes is a bit mysterious, and even though how it goes may seem baffling, the fact that it goes is more like going, going, gone! What if you took a look at your use of money and set up a plan for how you'd really like to see it spent in the future?

To begin, you'll need to take a look back and detail for a month where you spent your money and how much was spent. This is the raw data. Now develop a list of alternatives as to how you might do things differently for a month. Be creative; for example, you might notice from your notes that you have a large block of money that is spent on eating out each month but little for recreation, so one alternative might be to choose to cook and eat at home, in order to do something else special at the end of the month. If this seems helpful to you, try creating a month's budget.

> What was particularly eye opening to me was working with a budget for a year, I really looked hard at my monthly expenditures. Often I'm sold on 'It's only thirty dollars a month,' but when I look at that thirty dollars a month annually, that's $360. Reducing my

monthly utility expenditures by $10, $20, or $40 in a year can be saving me $120, $240, or $480. This was eye-opening to me. That's real money in real time.

Many people are amazed at what they have discovered and how empowered they felt to make changes. Ah, the power of a simple list.

Let's imagine that you feel confident in your grasp and use of money. You can follow the same process with any area where you wish to focus on change and find alternatives. First comes the object: look at the area where you realize you are stuck. "How much time, money, or affection am I devoting to this particular activity, endeavor, or relationship?" and then comes the list. "What other alternatives do I have?"

Developing the list isn't necessarily a solo venture. Invite a trusted friend to brainstorm ideas with you. If you are married, by all means work with your spouse, or gather the family around a whiteboard to look for possibilities and alternatives. Recently one of our client's families gathered four generations together to figure out alternative locations and possibilities for a big family reunion. They left feeling excited and full of adventure, as even the littlest was able to say what they wanted to do. Which by the way was "go fishing."

An Alternative Exercise

The Bible is full of examples of the alternatives different individuals choose and the consequences of their choices. In the life of David you can see amazing, faith-filled, gut-wrenching, character-drenched acts of bravery and kindness, love and nobility, and yet David made some profoundly wrong choices. What were the consequences of each of these? Look at some of the key junctures of his life, and make a list of alternatives that King David could have utilized "instead of ..." What was the consequence of not raising his son, Absalom, to love the Lord? How did his alternative choice affect other people?

The interesting piece about connecting these dots is how much we fall back into our understanding of self-observation, other-person perspective, and consequential thinking in order to come up with better alternatives to any given actions. The same thing can happen in your life as well. Where do you think Solomon got all his wisdom? Yes, of course it was a gift from God, but these activities and events of David's life weren't hidden in a corner. In a spoken culture like his, they would have been discussed at length. He undoubtedly learned a great deal from his father's triumphs as well as his mistakes.

Putting It All Together

When Internet providers began laying fiber optic cable, they were unaware of the true capacity of this new medium. With each improvement in technology they found to their astonishment that these cables just kept carrying more and more data, without laying new lines. In a sense they found fiber optics to be a gift that kept on giving.

Self-observation, other-person perspective, consequential thinking, and alternative thinking are four basic tools. Once learned and used, they are like those fiber optic cables in their ability to carry and process ever increasing amounts of useful interpersonal data upgrading life. The more we use them, and the more data we receive and process, the greater ease we find in deciphering, understanding, and responding appropriately.

From the therapist's chair: Again from the many years of working with individuals who are recovering from childhood trauma, both male and female, I realize how difficult applying alternative thinking may be for them in the beginning of the process. So many are accustomed to being told what to do, when to do it, and how to do it that they have not exercised the ability to make choices. Choosing alternatives and creating a pattern of alternative thinking may be just too scary for them to realize what they are missing in their lives. This is especially true of those with awesome creative talents, given to them by God: they are so stuck in what is routine that they fear trying to figure out how they might do anything differently. It is a point of risk taking to try an alternative way of thinking, a risk that, when the individual does step forward, they can truly be set free.

This poem has been on the wall at our office for many years. I am sorry I have no idea who penned the poem in the beginning, but thank you for doing so.

Risk

To laugh is to risk appearing a fool
To weep is to risk appearing sentimental
To reach out for another is to risk involvement
To expose feelings is to risk rejection
To place your dreams before the crowd is to risk ridicule
To love is to risk not being loved in return
To go forward in the face of overwhelming odds is to risk failure

But risks must be taken because the greatest
hazard in life is to risk nothing
The person who risks nothing does nothing,
has nothing, becomes nothing
He may avoid suffering and sorrow
But he cannot learn, feel, change, grow or love
Chained by his certitudes, he is a slave
He has forfeited his freedom
Only a person who takes risks is free.

A good note to end on … or is that to begin on?

Research on personal development indicates that those who work to build interpersonal maturity take more responsibility for their actions, have a better understanding of others, have better conflict resolution skills, and are more socially adjusted and helpful. They have better self-control and better frustration tolerance. As individuals develop interpersonal maturity, they usually experience a decrease in anxiety, sadness, and depression.

Wonderful, worthy outcomes are these, and how much would our world (and the church) be a better place if interest and pursuit of personal growth were universal? The hope for each of us is that the benefits of research aren't limited to the world or the church, but the benefits are very individual even personal. When our world seems so out of control, when the church is not the haven our soul craves, we almost feel that self-change is a small and insignificant thing. We forget that real change comes seldom from the top down but rather from the bottom up and that society is better when the people are better equipped. We may also forget that true change started with just one man, sent by God, to change people like you and me from the inside out.

I pray that this is your beginning and that you are able to remember and use what you now have learned, and that God will grow maturity within you to bless and build your life in Him and bless and beautify His bride, the church.

A Client's Perspective

"I don't know what's gotten into these students of mine! They left for break perfectly human and returned from Christmas vacation little monsters. I can hardly teach!"

I ranted a bit more and was just about to launch again when he interrupted, "It makes you wonder what happened to them over Christmas break."

I was stunned. The thought had never occurred to me that their hostile and erratic behavior could be a response to something other than me. I thought that they were all just particularly hateful and taking it upon themselves to make my job of teaching as difficult as humanly possible. "It makes you wonder what happened to them over Christmas break." I heard the echoes of that phrase reverberate off my mind's inner walls.

Most people shared my experience: a mostly happy Christmas, right? What if their Christmas was horrible, filled with anger, yelling, fighting, and sadness? I thought about some of the students and their families and realized this was a distinct possibility. I remembered the little girl who wanted nothing to do with any gifts from her mother, knowing they had been purchased with stolen credit cards. I began to realize that these children's behavior wasn't really directed at me; it was a response to their own conflicted emotions and family dramas. I just happened to be there.

When I realized that my students weren't out to get me and that their behavior could be understood by looking at what was going on in their lives, it began to change my teaching. As I grew in my ability to observe, my skill to work with and understand students increased dramatically. All this growth and understanding was a kind of side effect for a deeper and more profound change that I was pursuing.

My name is Burt, and this is one of the many client essays you'll read in this book. Our experiences are added and included because our stories are real and tell how we have moved forward in our lives. I hadn't come to the counselor's office to learn to observe students objectively. I came to get answers. I needed help. Why didn't my dating relationships go anywhere? Why was I depressed? *Who am I?*

Self-observation became an enormous window on my own behavior. I became a learner at family gatherings.

I watched, felt, and listened to my interactions with my parents and began to understand my own life's story. My student's weren't the only ones that needed compassion and understanding. It's been very hard, but I'm now judging myself less and understanding and accepting who I am more.

Just the other day in my journal I wrote, "I like myself." In case you missed the significance of those three words, they are huge! I didn't just go through a short patch of my life where I was down on myself; this is the first time in my life that I've ever really been able to say those words and have them feel true.

If you are reading this, there is a good chance that you are looking for answers in your own life. As one who has stood in your shoes, I want to encourage you that change is possible. My depression has lifted, and I am on a path of hope and healing. It is the desire of all who have contributed to this book that you will find the help you are looking for and the answers for your troubling questions. Know also that you are not alone. In your hand is a book full of lives that have walked the same path that you are starting now. We hope that our life stories will bring light to you in your journey.

From a Client's Perspective

The four principles of self-observation, other-person perspective, consequential thinking, and alternative thinking have helped me work through conflicts in my life. Before learning these principles, I had a difficult relationship with my children, spouse, and others. Since meeting with Dr. Silvey and learning these tools, I have seen my relationships grow in ways I never thought possible. I watched my children go from fearing me and being afraid to talking to me, opening up to me, and having heart-to-heart talks, many talks.

Self-observation is one of the hardest of these principles to accomplish, but I believe it is the most important. Since we are not mad at ourselves, the problem must be with the other person. However, the only people we can change are ourselves. We can't stop someone from calling us names, but we can choose not to let it get us angry.

Using other-person perspective has helped me to "not assume" but to really look at where another person is coming from. Did something happen earlier in the day or week, or is there a past hurt that may be driving her? If I can see a situation through her eyes, it becomes easier to understand her point of view and thus communicate more clearly to resolve differences.

Consequential thinking has helped me think things through more thoroughly than in the past. Will my words or actions cause someone to be hurt physically or emotionally? Will they live up to the standards I have set for myself? These questions help me respond more appropriately.

I have learned through developing alternative thinking to think of different ways to resolve conflicts in my every day life. For example, if I want to watch a program on TV but my spouse doesn't want to watch it, is there another program we both would like? Or can we work out an agreement to record one show and then take turns watching our shows?

I have helped my children and spouse learn these principles and have watched them work in their lives also. In the past, the yelling we experienced left all involved feeling angry, alone, and not cared for. We now resolve conflicts with calm and understanding, even when we don't agree. Our understanding of each other is deeper. We still have conflict in our relationships, but we work through them quicker, with less hurt, and a better understanding of each other's thought process. Thank you, Dr. Silvey!

Thoughts from Another Individual

When Dr. Silvey and I first spoke about self-observer, other-person perspective, and consequential and alternative thinking, I had a pretty good idea that they could help my life a great deal, but at the time I did not fully realize how much they would have helped me.

Other-person perspective helped immensely with my interpersonal relationships, especially in regards with my girlfriend of almost three years. When she and I would have "miscommunications," I would stop and see things from her point of view, and it helped me understand her, and thus we would work things out easily.

Consequential thinking has kept me from making mistakes that I am so glad I didn't have to learn from the hard way, if I would have survived at all.

Alternative thinking has helped me come up with solutions to problems that otherwise would have created a great deal of strife.

And finally, self-observation is the reason I am the person I am today. When I was younger, I began to self-analyze, and it helped me mature greatly.

Using these techniques has helped me greatly through life and with my relationships. I am teaching others so that they too will benefit from using self-observation, other-person perspective, and consequential and alternative thinking.

CHAPTER 6

RESEARCH BASIS FOR THE SEVEN STAGES OF DEVELOPMENT

A numbers of studies have been written on theories of development, some with and some without extensive research. Some have contributed to the overall growth in understanding of how individuals develop. The three most important and well-known studies have been by Jean Piaget (*Theory of Cognitive Development*), Eric Erickson (*Theories of Psychosocial Development*), and Lawrence Kohlberg ("Kohlberg's States of Moral Development"). In 1981, James Fowler wrote *Stages of Faith*, which is based on the early theories of development. Research written by Grant, Grant, and Sullivan, along with later research, was based on the theories of Piaget and Erickson.

In my training I was enormously fortunate to work with researchers who were developing treatment for individuals based on their maturity (California, 1966–1977). A large portion of time was devoted to developing an interview instrument to help determine an individual's level of awareness. From this research it became clear that there were stages of development and also at each stage different ways people coped. This was based on the research of Grant, Grant, and Sullivan in the 1950s. As I continued my training, I began seeing connections with how Scripture reflected the same developmental sequence for humanity. I began putting together ways to further development and also to identify barriers to growth and creating strategies to overcome them.

The Development of Interpersonal Maturity

The basic premise is that people create meaning from the world's complexity by organizing what they learn from their daily experience. They formulate a view of the world and use it to manage and adjust to life's situations so that they are able to meet their needs. This organization becomes a central point of reference from which they experience the world as well as their needs and expectations. It becomes their working philosophy of life, which the research calls "core." Relationship and communication are crucial in the development of this core. This interaction with others begins very simply and then continues to develop more complexity. This core becomes a sort of lens or grid through which the world is viewed. Individuals gravitate toward a state where their worldview solidifies and becomes resistant to change.

Normal development follows a pattern of increasing involvement with people, objects, and then social institutions. The effect of this natural progression is a sequential emergence of new perspectives (or various cores) throughout life, each more complex than at the previous stage, and at the same time incorporating previous coping strategies. When this normal pattern doesn't occur, the concept of core is very useful in understanding why. For example, how is it that individuals with similar traumatic experiences have very different responses? I see this frequently in my practice. Two people grow up in similarly abusive home environments; one is able to realize dreams of job and family, the other moves into addictive behaviors and never seems to be able to break free. The concept of core provides an explanation for this disparity as well as explanations for a way forward.

In addition, the theory presents seven successive states of development. Each stage is defined by a problem that must be solved to move on in development. An individual can become fixated or stuck at any stage for numerous reasons; for example, people's insecurities and anxieties create resistance to change, holding them back from growth. Other factors that cause fixation and strategies for getting unstuck will be discussed at some length in section three.

The section of this book that follows, "Seven Stages of Development," is based on the original research as it was further developed through the 1960s and 1970s and also connections that I have seen and recorded for moral spiritual development. As I became more familiar with this theoretical model, I was able to see how the Scriptures reflect the same developmental sequence.

Throughout my practice, this intensive work has been the basis for helping hundreds of individuals. Since the 1970s a silence has fallen over this research, and those familiar with these theories unfortunately, like myself, are getting older and retiring.

Wisdom Is like Gold, Timeless, Valuable, Easily Buried and Forgotten

It took two months just to record and load the *Atocha* with its precious cargo. When it set sail, this Spanish treasure ship was a regular floating Fort Knox. The trip to Spain was cut short by a detour straight to Davy Jones's locker, courtesy of a hurricane from which even its twenty-eight-ship escort couldn't protect it. Its loss nearly bankrupted the Spanish Government in 1622, and there the story ended, covered by mystery for 363 years. Discovered by treasure hunters in 1985, the hoard has an estimated worth above 450 million dollars.

Here is where it gets personal for me. I view these insights on human nature with a special reverence and see them as a treasure of incalculable value. That's why I devoted 1,500 hours of training to this research and hundreds of hours of interviews on the sequence of development. This research with profound implications was conducted by a staff at four different sites simultaneously in four different counties, at enormous financial investment by the National Institutes of Mental Health. What is left to show for all this? Well, perhaps only ten dusty copies in university libraries across the United States. It has all but disappeared except for an enormous box in my storage room. As I reference this research with therapists under my clinical supervision, they tell me that it is just not available and have urged me to let it be lost no more.

Implications and Opportunities for the Church

Americans have forgotten how to grow up. The average adult today has an emotional interpersonal maturity level equivalent to a 15- to 19-year-old. Most of you already have guessed that as you work with co-workers, talk with your neighbors, read the news, or watch TV. Sadder yet, and you probably already guess this as well, this includes the church. With all the riches of heaven at our disposal,

American Christians are awash in a poverty of insight. In a day desperate for depth, in a culture crying out for light, why are so many Christians grabbing for a bottle instead of a knife and fork, and choosing leaders just like them? The Father's heart is for each of His own to *grow up*.

The concept of core is also present and significant in Scripture, and the very same growth progression can be seen. God's goal, then and now, is to have His people shift the way that we see and interact with Him and take the growth steps that move us each deeper into relationship together.

His people perish for lack of knowledge. It is my hope and prayer that you will be aided in your own growth through these materials and in turn can be a light pointing from the nursery to full maturity in Christ.

Development Stage One

Question: Where do I stop and where do others begin?

Problem to be solved: Becoming aware that everything around me, including my mother and father, is not a part of myself.

The first stage is the awareness of separateness from self and everything else. The newborn does not see the self as separate from the world. That concept develops over time. Gradually the infant begins to treat people and things as non-self relievers of needs. The two parts of Stage One are (a) no one exists except for my need for food, and (b) others exist to meet all my other needs. In the first months there is little awareness of others. Later the mother becomes the center of my needs, and separation anxiety becomes highly prevalent. Unless some medical circumstances prevail, an infant will usually move on to the next stage of development.

Prior to birth the infant will store emotional memories. These emotional memories of loss or abuse may last unconsciously or consciously for a lifetime. During a session with a fourteen-year-old male, being seen for anger management, we began talking about his emotional brain. He told me that when his mother was pregnant with him, she would play a particular type of music. She played the music to help her grieve the loss of a baby prior to the client's birth, a boy baby who had died before him. The mother stopped playing the music at eight months of pregnancy, yet after my client's birth, whenever he heard that particular song, he would cry. Memories are stored prior to birth, and once the fourteen-year-old understood this concept, he was able to begin to process his feelings, including his anger.

What if an adult is stuck at this very first stage of development? Adults who are stuck here seem to operate as if the whole world is present to meet their needs. They have no perspective of the needs of others, and they will basically make no attempt to solve basic problems. Magical thinking is common among them, and they have little or no ability to postpone gratification. They operate as if they are the whole world. They distort life experiences and are unaware of the world around them. Their feelings easily overwhelm them. Even close relationships are distorted, so that they are the only one and the other person is an object to meet their needs. Such a person cannot submit to control or understand more than a primitive view of their environment.

The following is a list of characteristics of those individuals who are in Stage One development. Are any of these characteristics familiar to you? Both Bev and I can remember this stage of development for our kids. Our son had a strong way of expressing his needs and our daughter who had asthma expressed her needs differently. Neither of them stayed in Stage One very long.

Stage One List of Characteristics

1. I am my own god, my own world, and nothing of importance exists except me.
2. I am hungry; give me something to eat now.
3. That is pretty or fun; I want it now.
4. You are supposed to know what I feel and think without my signals.
5. I did not want to do that, so I am mad.
6. I am mad, sad, or happy, and I do not know why or how it changed.
7. People come and go; why can't they just be here for me?
8. There is nothing I can do to make things better; it is all up to you, so fix it now.
9. We are really one, so what I want, you want.
10. Life is really just magical.

It is 3:00 a.m., and the wail of a baby pierces through the darkened house. As parents stumble out of bed, instantly a list comes into their head that they begin to check off. *When was the last time I fed her?*

Hmmm, an hour ago; can't be that. What about changing? Just did that too. And as they reach baby, they begin to comfort and continue to problem solve: *Is she warm? Has the blanket slipped off, is she tangled in the blanket, or is the pacifier out of reach? Egad, hope it's not another earache!*

Little bundles of joy have no other way to communicate at this level but to use their voices, often loudly. The infant signals, and skilled hands and brains go to work to mind read and problem solve. Blessed sleep becomes a great reward to weary parents when the riddle is solved and they can flop back into bed.

What is going on in the mind of the child? Probably something like "I have a need; fix it for me now!" The magical aspect of all this, of course, is that with very limited ability to communicate, and this mostly by crying, infants do communicate their need. Soon parents have attended to and soothed them, and it is as if their signal summons arms and cooing that take care of all problems.

At an early age infants are aware of sensations, but not actually aware of their body and the control that they will someday have over it. For all they know, they are connected to this outside pair of arms and hands and enormous face that looms over their very small world and upward view. Infants have little awareness that they are separated from everything else around them. They are one with the world. The idea that their body is a space ship that will someday maneuver them about in this wide world will develop in time. The first glimmers of this awakening separateness or autonomy is when they begin to treat people and things as relievers of their tension, basically, an object to meet their needs and want.

Development Stage Two

Question: Is there anything I can do that will make it easier to get what I need or want?

Problem to be solved: Is life more than my needs and how I feel right now?

The second stage of development does differentiate to a degree between self and non-self. So now I have a problem of how to control things to get what I want. At this time children become aware of how people or things can block them from getting what they want. People begin to be seen as a means to the end of getting what they want, so they may become highly dependent or aggressive.

Although these children have grown past omnipotence, they are still at a very simple and immature stage of life. Their approach to life is that something is wrong with others when their own needs are not being met. As adults they will view others as either givers or withholders. They may have primitive social techniques, making demands instead of requests and not understanding why their demands are not being met. Such individuals do not have an emotional recognition yet do react emotionally toward others who do not meet their needs. Their anxiety is intense when they feel deprived. As a result, their way to cope is manipulation, a tendency to use people as a way to get what they want with no care for the other's feelings or the consequences.

These individuals have very poor self-control and either blow up or withdraw on the basis of their feelings. Their relationship with others is superficial and with little or no remorse for past or present behavior. Others see these individuals as unstable, unpredictable in nature, and often unreachable.

In my career I have been in a number of jails and prisons to administer inmate evaluations. Many were stuck in Stage Two development. They are antisocial and narcissistic, with very little other-person perspective. They try to manipulate others to get what they want in immature and impulsive behaviors. Others remain dependent on others as in a childlike way. They are anxious and depressed and need others to take care of them.

Consider Jean Piaget's most famous study. Two identical glasses are filled with equal amounts of water. A child agrees that it is the same amount of water, but when one glass is poured into a taller, thinner glass the child will say the taller, thinner glass has more water. When the water is again poured into the original glass, the child will say they are equal again. The child's level of development determines her perception. Without this ability to simplify, life would be overwhelming. As children get older and have a more developed understanding, they will agree it is the same amount of water no matter what you pour the water into.

Sam's Story

Sam was born in a small town in Oregon, close to Portland. His parents were both immature adults and prone to addictions. His father left his mother and him when he was very young. His mother would have different men in the home and introduce each one as his new dad.

His mother abused alcohol, leading her to become a serious alcoholic. When she was drinking, she was physically abusive to Sam. Sam learned how to survive on his own and even as a young child would break into neighbors' homes, mainly to get sweets and toys. Oregon Child Protective Services referred Sam to me as his therapist when he was eight years old. Sam did not trust adults and was mainly at Stage Two in development. He had trouble in school, as he would get angry easily and yell at the teachers and staff. Often he would fight with other students.

During our sessions together we worked on simple consequential thinking skills and the need for rules to keep him from trouble. Sam got into trouble again, and this time he was sent to a residential treatment facility. Sam was ruled by his feelings, especially anger. He did not trust people and would manipulate others to get what he wanted from them in an immature way. The things he got were only a temporary solution to make him feel better. Sam remained at Stage Two development into his adult life.

I later had contact with Sam and as the story continues was able to encourage him, along with his residential counselor. While there, Sam had trouble in the beginning and would act out. He began to learn the rules and roles to stay out of trouble. More important, he learned that people genuinely cared for him and were not going to hurt or abuse him. Sam began to learn that the rules helped him get what he wanted, but in his thinking, the rules are magical: "I follow the rules; why didn't I get what I wanted?" It's like the child who says please and then asks, "So why can't I have the cookie?"

Sam was able to graduate from the treatment facility when he was eleven years old and was placed into foster care. I saw Sam again when he was twenty-nine years old, and he still had very little understanding of SOCA. He was staying out of trouble with the law, as he had gained a little use and understanding of consequential thinking.

Jessica's Story

Jessica pouts and sulks when she doesn't get her way. She picks men as husbands who will appease her, and when they don't, she moves on, and her choices have led her to husband number five. As long as you're useful, you're in; but setting boundaries usually results in a hefty heave-ho, off the plank you go. It isn't just with husbands either. She won't talk to her parents, and they've given up on her, and she goes from church to church, job to job, agency to agency looking for the help she needs to get out of her latest crises. She continually creates turmoil for herself and then wonders aloud to all who will listen at how unfair and cruel the world has been to her. The sad part is that she really believes it! She's on the lookout for "nice" people to listen and help her. Unfortunately they often do, and Jessica has radar for people that she can use. For Jessica, codependency is her idea of a match made in heaven; it's what she unconsciously aims for in her relationships. She is firmly stuck in Stage Two and by choice probably will remain there long-term.

List of Characteristics Stage Two

1. In relationships with peers, the individual is demanding and alienated and will blame others as a scapegoat.
2. The individual's relationships are described only in terms of whether others "give to" or "deny."
3. The individual does not connect the giving or denying response of others to his own behavior.
4. The individual never seems to know what is expected of her.
5. Actions of others are either unpredictable or deemed irrelevant and are viewed as the principal cause of frustrations.
6. The individual is relatively unaware of his impact on others.
7. The individual is able to feel only her own wants and frustrations. She does not perceive others' needs and concerns.
8. The individual has little awareness of the need to contribute anything in order to bring about giving responses from others.
9. The individual is characterized by acting out hostility.
10. The individual's self-image is described only in terms of others frustrating him or what he wants others to do for him.
11. The individual is relatively unaware of social norms.
12. The individual has little or no idea that there are consequences to her behavior.

The Old Testament is full of examples of people and the world getting stuck at this Stage Two development. Genesis 6:5 says, "The Lord saw how great man's wickedness on the earth had become, and that every inclination of the thoughts of his heart was only evil all the time." Genesis 18:20 (see verses 19–28) indicates that Sodom and Gomorrah were also totally evil and were destroyed. Joseph's own brothers sold him into slavery. While Moses was on the mountain, even after all the miracles in Egypt, the Israelites build a calf of gold as the god who saved them from Egypt. The children of Israel constantly complained because they did not get what they wanted when they wanted it. At the early part of Stage Two development, people determine what is right and wrong, good or evil based on their needs, desires, wants and impulses.

Today Christians who are stuck in Stage Two look to the church and to God to meet their needs. They can be both dependent and explosive according to the circumstance. They do not comprehend the need for growth and understanding of Scripture, as there is still magical thinking present. They are inconsistent in church attendance unless the church is helping them, or they seek out another church that is more supportive of their needs. They do not develop real relationships with other members of the church, only superficial relationships as long as their needs are met. Often children who are raised in addictive families, even Christian families, do not get beyond Stage Two development. The children grow up and often become demanding, controlling, and abusive as adults. They may attend a church to make an appearance, "look good," and impress people.

Some children who are adopted have great difficulty developing attachments (Stage One). The child may struggle with the next stage because of his or her belief that no one is to be trusted. They suspect that even the adoptive parents will abandon them. Basic trust of the parents is necessary for trust development in God. Those individuals who seek counseling and support groups and who continue in their own development may gradually build trust in God and others.

A church with a ministry program to street people has the hard task of discerning when an individual may be using manipulation or truly allowing God to work in their life. When Bev and I were volunteer youth ministry coordinators for a small church in California, we had several street kids who would come to church activities. They were ministered to and over time grew in maturity and trust toward others and us. Some even began to trust that God did really love them in spite of themselves. The transition between Stage Two and Stage Three is often a result of the consequences of violating the rules— whether family or societal rules. The pain from the consequences, either emotional or physical, may direct the individual to focus on the rules that are broken. The individual may receive the discipline only in rebellion, because Stage Two individuals still want what they want when they want it.

I remember a young man who had lived his life as he wanted to with little consideration of the consequences. He was arrested, and this time none of his family rescued him; he was incarcerated. The family stood strong while recognizing they had enabled their son to stay stuck in Stage Two development. The mother in particular began to change and grow into maturity as a result of this difficult situation. Sometimes it is a hard pathway from Stage Two to Stage Three development, yet the benefit of continuing through the stages could be "release for generations to come." Do you want to be the mature model for yourself and your family?

Development Stage Three

Question: Do I have to follow the rules, and who makes the rules?

Problem to be solved: Can I make my own decisions and choose what I want or do not want to do?

The Third Stage of development is the integration of rules and the roles that people play in giving or withholding what they want. At this point rules become the way to get what we want and a means to satisfaction. The magic changes from people to the rules ("I said please"). Rules now have control, and people have different roles in what they do. The same rules apply to all situations. If the rules are too harsh or inconsistent, then fear and resentment develop.

At Stage Three the questions of knowledge and goodness are raised. Rules determine life and outcome; rules are to be followed or broken. Different rules determine different outcomes. Who makes the rules? Can I make my own rules? How do rules work? Who enforces the rules? Why do I have to obey the rules?

Rules become more complex and hard to understand while at the same time being simplified down to only a few and integrated as the only way. It is the way the rules are organized that becomes more consistent and stable. Consider those who believe that others will use them to their own advantage, so they develop their own formula for dealing with others. These people may devote many hours to community service or to church work; their purpose is to satisfy or meet the requirements of the rules. One of the rules may be "I need others to see me as loving, serving, and willing to help at all times." In a stressful or threatening situation they may regress to emotional outbreaks at others. When the stress is removed, they may return to community service as if nothing had happened. With long-term observation the pattern will repeat again and again until the underlying motives are discovered and changed.

Terri's Story

Terri was an excellent athlete, playing a variety of sports at an early age. Her mother received acknowledgment and attention from others' parents for Terri's abilities. Her mother continued to push Terri to practice more and work out longer and harder, to the point of not spending any time with her childhood friends. Terri was highly critical of herself when she did not meet her expectations, especially in gymnastics. Her dream was to participate in the Olympics. A severe leg injury ended her dream and her sports career. She was lost and depressed and contemplated suicide. Unaware of the emotional trauma Terri was experiencing, her mother continued to push her until she realized the severity of the loss. Terri and her mother sought professional counseling and began to form new conclusions about life.

To an adult stuck at this stage, the world is a series of rigidly organized rule-bound relationships. The concern is "What can I do to make people respond to me the way I want?" The question is, "Exactly what is expected of me, and what do I need to do to avoid problems?" The person can be the dependent, conforming type (Dependent Personality) or the one who tries to manipulate the rules (Confidence Man). Either you trust everyone as more powerful and do what they want, or you trust no one and manipulate the rules to get what you want. The adult who functions at this level becomes anxious when he does not know what the rules are or whether the rules have changed. He may spend a lifetime "trying out" different roles with rules and never find satisfaction or peace within the role. Life becomes a play in which one individual is all of the actors and the director. The Stage Three individual will put on the mask of the role to please the one who is directing. Or the Stage Three individual becomes the director and manipulates everyone else in the life play to get what he or she wants. Which are you—the all-encompassing actor or the manipulating director?

Stage Three List of Characteristics

1. The individual is able to play prescribed stereotyped roles.
2. The individual presents himself as satisfied with his mode of living, rejecting the notion of needed change for himself.
3. The individual is most comfortable when the external structure is clearly defined and consistent. She will often get stuck on the familiar.
4. The individual will change purported values if expedient; i.e., she has little internalized end result.
5. The individual does not challenge means as being at fault, when he fails to achieve his end result.
6. The individual underestimates the complexity of others.

7. The individual cannot understand the needs, feelings, and motives of others as being different from his own.

8. There is minimal differentiation among others. The individual can distinguish some roles but cannot perceive needs and feelings different from her own.

9. The individual assumes that a very few rules, formulae, or techniques will handle all interpersonal interactions.

10. The individual looks for structure in new situations so he can function (apply his formula) without discomfort, interference, or punishment.

11. Who are they? does not occur to him. His description of others will be superficial, restricted, and lacking in depth.

12. The individual describes others in terms of stereotyped, roles-related responses such as "popular," "athletic," "successful," or "wealthy."

13. The individual does not expect behavior and intent of others to differ from her own; therefore, she often seriously errs in predicting their response to her.

14. The individual's thinking and learning processes are highly concrete. He has little motivation for integrating, interpreting, abstracting, or resolving information.

15. The individual has little to no awareness that needs and feelings of others differ from his own.

Much of the Old Testament consists of rules and roles, especially Exodus and Judges. Before Moses' experience with God and the burning bush, Moses was a conformist. He conformed to the rules in Egypt until he was forty and killed the Egyptian. He conformed to Jethro, his father-in-law, until he was eighty years old and saw the burning bush. Even at that point Moses was anxious and insecure, asking, "Who am I, and what if they don't believe me?" When the children of Israel were in the desert, they were like Stage Two adults, complaining and demanding.

God knew what humanity needed, so He gave us a set of rules that we could live by and continue our development. The children of Israel did not accept the rules or role of Moses but rather complained about what they believed they wanted. In the book of Judges the rules had been established, but they did not have a leader to direct them. As a result, the Israelites intermarried with other nations and worshipped the images of Baal and Asherah. They went back to Stage Two development. Every time they had a new judge, they followed his rules, and when he died, they would return to their previous behavior, doing evil in the sight of the Lord.

Even today people follow leaders or pastors as long as they are in control, sometimes to the point of death, as in Jonestown. Often when a charismatic pastor leaves a church, the church stops growing and falls apart. This is also true of some of the media churches and their followers. I have seen a number of young adults who become like the individual or group of individuals that they were hanging out with at the time. When they are with one group, they will act like others within the group. When with the partygoers, they drink and get rowdy like the other partygoers do. When the teens go to church, they sing the praise songs and talk about the Bible and their walk with God just like others attending with them. When asked who they believe they are, they often cannot tell you. This is called Stage Three "chameleon:" "I change who I am to be like those around me so that I can fit in."

Christians today who are stuck at the Stage Three level of development can be very critical of others. They want structure and a style of worship that is familiar. It is hard for them to grow beyond what a church has been like for years. So in many ways the church does not meet the needs of the people, thus creating an atmosphere in which the church does not grow. Church rules (spoken or unspoken) to which the people are expected to obey are common if the pastor has not grown beyond Stage Three development. Structure is more important than growth, and differences are not seen as strengths but as a hindrance toward the preset goals.

Christians who are raised in the Stage Three church are often naïve. They need to be seen as Christ like but do not have the personal maturity to make good choices about others. Often I have seen a Christian family take in people they desire to help, only to find out that these people have stolen from them, used drugs, and even initiated the family's children into drugs or criminal behavior. The problem is not taking in these individuals, but at Stage Three the purpose or motive behind the action is more to fulfill a family role, or perceived family role, not necessarily the leading of the Holy Spirit. The family may not have spent time seeking what God would have them do. Stage Three Christians are more stuck in the should's or the should-not's and consequently lack discernment. I do appreciate their conviction in doing what they believe is the right thing to do; but without the development of godly discernment, their decisions may cause more problems.

Individuals who have moved toward Stage Four often slide back into Stage Three when placed in a role, usually by someone close to them. They may not quite have the strength to say no to the assigned role and will continue in the role until it again becomes too much. Stronger individuals will resist the rules and rebel against them. As individuals learn to say, "No, this is not where I choose to be or what I choose to do," they will make the transition into Stage Four and stay there longer. Hopefully, they can progress into a deeper Stage Three–Stage Four transition without being disrespectful and harming relationships.

From Bev: "I remember a situation that I faced while being a youth coordinator. My young son had been sick with various colds and earaches, and it had been a long, cold winter that year. While I was finishing something at the church for the next youth activities, a well-meaning yet persistent pastor stopped me and asked, 'Why aren't you going on the choir tour with the youth? We must have a woman go with them.'

"Try as I might, he would not let it go until I said, 'You know I just can't, and Murl and I will have to pray hard before I can say yes to going.' I do believe this was my first step into a solid Stage Four development phase. As I matured more and progressed more in my development, I surely learned not to be pressured into saying yes if I truly believed that God was saying no!"

What happens when someone who has been in Stage Four slips back into Stage Three? Maybe she has been promoted to a supervisory role and within a short time has become harsh and demanding of others. She will not consider the other person's circumstances and may change a schedule without notice. She considers the supervisory role as a way to be in charge. It becomes difficult for her to step out of the supervisory role, and family members are often treated more like employees than loved ones. Males more than females have a difficult time with the work-to-home transition. I have found that praying before reentry into the home is vital.

In adolescence, teens may follow the rules in public situations at school or with the coaches, but at home they will talk back to the parents and defend what they want to do. The rules have lost their magic, and the reward is not significant enough for them to care. Teens can cooperate with the parents but may very well decide that the rules just do not benefit the role they want for themselves, healthy or unhealthy. The question of "Who am I, and am I good enough?" pushes the individual toward Stage Four identity issues. When the teen can finally see that the rules and roles are a benefit, he will try out different scenarios within the home to see which best fits him, and then he may move forward into Stage Four.

Alice's Story

When I first started seeing Alice, she was a thirty-year-old who had intense guilt and shame and felt that she could never be "good enough." She was a rescuer and tried to take care of everyone. Her husband was immature, so she felt responsible to work and take care of the home. He worked outside the home but did not help at home or with the two children. She made sure they got to their appointments and went to school for the meetings with teachers. She was responsible for taking them to their respective sports events.

Alice felt depressed and blamed herself for why her marriage was more like parallel living than a relationship. We began to work on what it meant from Scriptures to love herself, as the Bible says to love your neighbor as yourself. She began to see that she did not even know who she was as a person but rather as what she needed to do to be loved. She did not have female friends or go to a women's Bible study. She attended church alone with her children.

It is interesting how many adults get stuck in this stage of development, especially Christians who are raised in a rigid rules and roles home. They either submit to the authority or they rebel against it. Many will revert back to Stage Two: "I'm going to do just what I want to do."

Alice began to understand that she was stuck in her feelings and the need to please or take care of others not as a choice but to avoid feeling guilty. She also began to experience the love of God and not His judgment. Alice began to express her needs to her husband, which was very difficult.

In her childhood years, Alice was raised in a strong Christian home that emphasized rules and that God was more of a judge who would give consequences for breaking His laws or her parents' rules. Alice began to grow and to mature as she made changes in her life. Her husband noticed the changes, and he began to change too, coming to some of the children's appointments. We worked on self-observer and other-person perspective, and Alice was able to work on her own identity in Christ, an identity not based on performance. Always before, when she would go to a Bible study, she would interpret her growth on performance standards; now she sees how the study promoted spiritual development. She began to experience Scripture that declares, "If you know the truth, the truth will set you free indeed." Alice has moved through to Stage Four and is developing toward Stage Five characteristics.

Stage Four Development

Question: How do I know what I want to do and not get in trouble for what I do? How am I different than the roles I live out?

Problem to be solved: I need to be more consistent with who I am and what I want, rather than reverting back to former beliefs.

The fourth stage of development, often called Separation and Individuation, is often a series of conflicts with others in deciding who I am and what I want. "Is this really me, and what do I do now?" At this point there is a more developed objective view of self, with growth in relationships with others and an awareness of social influences. One begins to accept the impossibility of controlling others and wants to have a clearer perspective of one's own life and the confidence to control one's world.

The desire is now to see yourself as others see you, as well as a desire to be an individual. An identity begins to develop that is more than that of an observer or victim of life. The question "Who am I?" begins to develop, and role playing is more of the question "Is this me?" There is still the problem of integration and consistency with the new identity. Often this leads to feelings of inadequacy or not being good enough. There is need for acceptance and approval, yet we are conflicted with the desire to make our own choices.

As an adult this is a difficult place, having developed physically but not having integrated the new awareness of oneself and really not having developed self-esteem. At this stage, an adult may feel guilt for not measuring up to the person he or she wants to be. This may lead to psychosomatic symptoms and a number of addiction issues (including drugs, alcohol, or sex). Expression of an identity may lead to acquiring things—a nice car, house, spouse, etc.—but this still does not meet the need for a personal identity. Emotions may run amuck during the search for identity. If confronted, people may lose control and become explosive. This is the time when they may revert back to old victim-style withdrawn patterns of behavior or patterns aggression or anger.

From Bev: "I was twenty-eight when I realized things were not as I wanted them to be, nor was I who I believed God wanted me to be. There were few self-help books to help along the way, but I knew I had to change me. I began simply by taking a piece of paper and folding it in half. On one side I began to write down the things I had been told about myself in childhood or the characteristics I thought I displayed. On the other side of the paper I began to write down the truths about who God says I am, the characteristics He has developed in me, and the gifts He was revealing to me. This process took some time, and I had to cycle back often to what is God's truth about me. The process prompted an in-depth study of *The Character of God*, by A. W. Tozer, an author whose wisdom could have only come from the Holy Spirit. I have a very well-worn copy on my bookshelf and review and delight in each page often. I pray, as I will turn seventy this year, to continue this developmental growth journey until I enter into heaven."

List of Stage Four Characteristics

1. The individual shows evidence of discomfort or conflict when he does not measure up to his own (not his peers') expectations.
2. The individual wants recognition from those she admires—recognition of her uniqueness, potential, or accomplishments.
3. The individual expects a parent–child type of relationship with authorities or boss, focused on the issue of control.
4. The individual tests people to see if they really are who they say they are.
5. The individual is able to perceive that self and others can change over time.
6. The individual is able to relate to adults on an equalitarian basis. He can relate to other adults other than on a child–parent basis.
7. The individual evaluates herself along certain dimensions (size, intelligence, appearance, social skills) as better or worse than others.
8. The individual shows some capacity to delay response to immediate stimuli. He can ask himself, "How will I feel later if I act this way now?"
9. The individuals see themselves and want others to see them as non-average, unique, different from others.

10. The individual wants to get ahead and make something of herself. She wants to have status and prestige.
11. The individual has potential for considerable insight into meanings, dynamics, and cause-and-effect reasoning.

Peter's Story

Peter was raised in a small town and went to a community church with his family. As a child and preteen he was compliant and did okay in school. During his older teen years, he started spending time with guys who were more rebellious and were known for using drugs. Peter was arrested with his friends, and his parents thought their job was to be stern and strong with him. At fifteen years of age, Peter along with two of his friends ran away and joined a group of street people in downtown Seattle. Peter continued his lifestyle of drugs and living on the streets until he was twenty-five. A decade of drug use, improper eating, and living on the street took a toll, and Peter developed some serious side effects. With few options, Peter agreed to enter Life Change, a successful Christian program for addicts. Peter accepted the reality that he needed help, lots of help, and was very successful at Life Change. Today, he serves the Lord and is moving forward to be the man God intended for him to be before his own choices derailed him.

As young Christians at Stage Four, many individuals walk away from their faith, indicating, "This is not for me, this is not me." David is an example of a young man who made a decision to believe and did not fall away when he became King David. He had confidence in God even against the giant, Goliath. On the other side, Saul took matters into his own hands after Samuel had told him to destroy Amalek and everything there, both human and animal. Saul listened to his men and then blamed them for sparing Agag, the king of Amalek, and saving the best of the animals and possessions. (1 Samuel 15:20–24). Christ's disciples struggled with what to do after Christ was crucified, they went fishing until Christ appeared to them and told them to "follow me" (John 21:19) Christians often struggle with making their relationship with Christ personal. They can also struggle with the questions: "How do I know that this is the right god for me? People talk about different gods. Can I choose any of them? Do I need to choose just one? It is like choosing one wife out of the many. Why be faithful to just one?"

Christians today who are stuck at the Stage Four level of development often struggle with the church and sometimes with Scripture telling them how to live or what to do in their lives. They often bounce back and forth between rules and roles and outright rebellion. They evaluate how others live and do not see a consistency in others' lives, so they decide being a Christian does not have value or meaning to them. They further develop a negative self-image and believe they do not meet the standards set by others or by the Bible. Although attending church, the rest of the week they live the way they want to. This may include addictions or other rebellious behavior.

Christian teens whose parents divorce may develop intensely rebellious behavior. Girls may become sexually active, and boys may be defiant, especially if they are not involved with both parents equally. They may use the problems between the parents to manipulate them and get what they want from each parent.

Christians who raise their children with strong rules and roles may have difficulty allowing their teen children to separate out from them and begin to become their own persons. David Brinkley asked the advice columnist Ann Landers about questions she received from readers. She said that one she received the most was "What is wrong with me?" Today, one would only have to look at any one of the numerous social network media to find a pervasive theme of "Who am I?" "Am I important enough?" What is wrong with me, so that no one cares?" In both of our practices we have seen this pattern again and again: Parents prescribed roles and the rules for their teen without any input from the teens. The teens cannot respect or adhere to the rules, so they begin to believe their parents are wrong, and then they struggle with being a part of the family. Usually some form of rebellion follows.

A healthy, creative way to establish the rules of the home is to consider each member of the family and what gifts God has given to each of them. A family unit built on respect given and received and respect for others will greatly enhance the communication of the whole. Then the family can use these insights to make rules that will encourage these gifts, not discourage them by placing individuals in boxes. We cannot serve our Lord if we are caught up in the box that someone else has declared is us.

Sometimes peer influences send the message, "Do what you have to in order to get what you want." I have seen many children and remember in particular two pastor's sons who were raised in a rigid rules and roles structured home. The boys became very rebellious, beginning around age fifteen and sixteen, and the rebellion continued into young adulthood. Unfortunately, one boy went to prison for robbery and the other for rape. Years later the boy convicted of robbery came to the office and told me how he had truly accepted Christ into his life and the changes that prison and his new commitment to Christ had brought into his life.

Individuals in their late teens and early twenties are usually in Stage Four. It is difficult for teens when they dream about their successes and then fail to meet the high standard they have set for themselves. On a popular TV show it is obvious in the early auditions that individuals had their minds set on winning and to their surprise were eliminated after the first round. Their emotions take over, and they become overwhelmingly sad and sometimes angry.

Athletes who were excellent in their small high school may find themselves unable to make the first string for their college freshman year. They often quit their sport because they feel, "I'm not good enough!" They may feel a need to prove themselves and begin acting out in risky behaviors. The need to prove oneself is very common in Stage Four behaviors, even in negative ways. Behaviors such as out drinking anyone else can lead to negative consequences, from alcohol poisoning to auto accidents to arrests.

Adults who are Stage Three until they reach thirty-five to forty-five years of age and then begin seeking personal life evaluations often have midlife transition issues or even a serious midlife crisis. Even as Christians, these individuals may experience divorce or make unexplained career changes while telling others, "It just wasn't me."

One such individual, a highly successful executive, left his lucrative job suddenly and began his own business. Unfortunately, he neglected to think ahead and plan adequately. The venture was not successful, and he became increasingly depressed and failed to care for himself or his family. Only after he sought counseling did he discover the gifts and qualities God had given him and turn his life and the life of his family around.

Some individuals reach Stage Four by finding their identity while answering the question "Who am I?" After their initial growth they often become complacent and settle for the status quo. This is how 80 percent of the adult population stays at lower emotional interpersonal maturity levels of a 15- to 19-year-old or less. They still have trouble managing their feelings and struggle to understand other people, especially in marriage. When they get stuck, they often divorce and continue to have interpersonal problems. One court-referred couple came to the office who had found success in business but fought with each other as if they were young teenagers. They never did settle their differences, even though one proclaimed to be a Christian.

The transition issue between Stage Four and Stage Five is most often over more stable identity. The individual still struggles with having a consistent sense of his or her identity. An underdeveloped identity is no match when circumstances and emotions intensify and often will trigger regression to an earlier developmental stage. Many adults who have matured to Stage Four and Stage Five may react to others, rather than respond to them in constructive ways. They often try to prove their point, rather than listening to the other person with openness and seeking clarification. Their tone of voice often gets intense. A recent statistic I read indicated that the vast majority of adults struggle with this regression even when they have been displaying mature behaviors.

During this transition the more time individuals spend in Stage Five, the less often they are reactive, and life is less intense. There is more stability in their life. The key to this change is becoming more aware of the things that are the triggers and working on those triggers by being more self-observant. The Stage Five individual no longer has to be right all the time and has become aware of and open to differences.

Paul's Story

Paul was raised in a strong Christian home where his dad was a pastor and really believed in "spare the rod and spoil the child." Paul first came in for counseling as a sixteen-year-old rebellious adolescent. He would sneak out of his house at night to spend time with his friends; of course his father had told him not to. He had gone through Stage Three and had decided he was not a Christian. Now he was just trying to decide who he was and where he wanted to spend time. In Paul's counseling sessions we would talk about whose life it was and what kind of life he wanted. We went over self-observer, other-person perspective, consequences, and alternatives, and he was beginning to admit that his choices were not only affecting him but others around him as well.

At seventeen Paul was just beginning to develop his understanding when he and a friend entered a 7-Eleven store. Paul's friend pulled a gun and robbed the store, killing the clerk in the process. Paul did not know this was going to happen, yet he did not leave and was arrested as an accomplice to robbery and murder. He was sentenced to seven years. While in prison he got involved in prison ministries and began to develop a strong relationship with Christ and other Christians. He taught others about SOCA and grew himself as they learned.

Paul was released from prison after the seven years. He found a good job, married, and had a child. He continues to volunteer in the prison ministry to tell others about his choices and their consequences. One afternoon, Paul brought his son to the office and thanked me for what he had learned in those sessions so long ago. We both were able to thank God for His mercy and grace in our development. Paul had moved from his rebellious Stage Four into Stage Five and even Stage Five–Six.

Development Stage Five

Question: How do I continue to develop and become a stronger person in the Lord?

Problem to be solved: What is holding me back from continuing to grow or taking me back to more immature thoughts, feelings, and behaviors?

The fifth stage is the development of more self-observation and personal growth. The individual can consider past, present, and future. At Stage Five the past is used as a place to remember, and then these memories or experiences become a foundation to learn more about oneself. The future has a hope as the individual has developed more self-confidence. Then the present is experienced with more consistency even in the ever-changing circumstances. Emotions can be experienced but no longer control behavior as in the earlier stages.

Alternatives can be explored, so there is insight into the choices, not reactions to the moment.

The individual may maintain roles, but only those that are appropriate for the situation. The individual is able to shift roles and still reflect his personal identity beyond the role. For the first time there is noticeable appreciation for others who have their own ideas and desires. The individual is beginning to see things as more complex, where he can understand both objective and subjective points of view. The individual's thoughts and feelings are understood and managed. True other-person perspective is developing.

As an adult there is no longer the intense struggle of identity. Other people's happiness or sorrow is experienced, and the individual can develop some boundaries and not be submerged with them. The individual is developing empathy. There is a greater tolerance for differences and ambiguity in others. There still may be some anxiety about who is the real me or who I am to become. There is more understanding of differences and complexity than before, both in the self and in others.

Christians at Stage Five are more consistent in their identity in Christ. They want to develop and grow, read their Bible, and attend Bible studies and are more able to share with others their love of God. As a Christian, they are experiencing the deeper meaning of life, as well as life's dependence on the relationship with God.

When we consider the life of the apostle Paul, we view his development from a strong desire to live to an extreme by rules. As he met and developed a relationship with Christ, his identity in Christ solidified;

so did his tolerance for differences in others. He developed good boundaries and was able without judgment to walk away from those leaders who were stuck in the law. Paul moved from Stages Three, Four, and Five into Stage Six.

Eric's Story

A pastor from Central Washington, Eric, made an appointment after revealing his sex addiction and an affair with a member of his church. He grew up in a Christian home and had a strong desire to follow the Lord. He became addicted to pornography as a teenager and had not been able to break the bondage. He worked hard in developing his boundaries with his thoughts and feelings. He then began to develop better self-control. He was able to stop his thoughts and the images in his mind as he took every thought captive. Believe me, it took Eric a long journey with God's grace and mercy to overcome his addiction. Eric is now free to be the pastor God desires him to be, forming men's groups within the church who are learning the tools of SOCA and boundaries. He moved to Stage Five and was more able to truly say, "Christ has set me free."

Stage Five Characteristics

1. The individual is able to be more aware of self and others before choosing a behavior and takes action to avoid problems.
2. The individual is aware of feelings and can express them and does not let those feelings take control.

3. The individual has empathy for others and can set boundaries so that what is happening for others does not affect her as in earlier stages, and she does not lose control over her boundaries with others as often.
4. The individual can consider the consequences of actions and find the best alternative.
5. The individual can look at the past as an aid in making decisions in the present.
6. The individual is able to shift goals and behavior to fit changes in demands from the external world.
7. The individual responds to others in terms of their healthy integrity.
8. The individual can disagree with others and respect the differences without making the differences a problem.
9. Others describe the individual as displaying leadership qualities.
10. The individual is capable of a goal-oriented process with follow-through.
11. The individual relates to others in a selective and non-compulsive way.

Christians at Stage Five can be stable in relationships at church, as they recognize and tolerate individual differences. They are seen as emotionally stable, even in the midst of crises. Scripture is better understood as a way to help develop a relationship with God. In a discussion about what a particular scripture means, the individual can discuss different interpretations and be open to others. Styles of worship are seen as different ways people express their relationship with God. At Stage Five, they are more able to make changes and still have an inner peace. The circumstances in life are managed and do not interfere with their relationship with God. The individual is able to assume leadership roles without becoming too involved with the problems of others. There is a separateness of self between the role and the expectation of the role from others.

An angry adolescent from a dysfunctional family chose to come to therapy to work on his own development. This young man was in Stage Three and Stage Four. When he first came in, he really did not know who he was or what he wanted to do. As we went over SOCA, he began to discover how to develop his inner self and not just react to the outside. He learned how to deal with the losses he experienced in his life and build confidence that he could have a good life. After college graduation, he interviewed for an impressive job. The interviewer said because of his maturity he was given the position He is still aware he needs to continue to grow personally and spiritually.

The progression from Stage Five to Stage Six is a deeper awareness of the internal process and consistency as a result. As awareness deepens, people are able to process and consider what they are thinking and feeling and the choices that are available. They can respond and be considerate of others, while managing and maintaining their own belief system.

Development Stage Six

Question: What does it mean to have Christ-likeness?

Problem to be solved: My inconsistencies are fewer, and I strive to continue my growth in my relationship with God, with others, and within myself.

Stage Six development is an exciting time of becoming the individual God has intended you to be from the beginning. Stage Six is a time to discover the gifts and talents that God has instilled within you. The roles, although they exist (father, mother, parent, pastor, and teacher) do not determine your identity even when moving from one role to another. The old saying is accurate: "Wherever I go, there I am." As the true identity is expressed, the rules and the roles do not determine the expressions or behavior. There is a continuous integration of past, present, and future. These individuals are able to have and maintain healthy relationships. They are able to allow the inconsistencies in others and their shifting behavior and still be friends with them. When placed in a leadership position, the individual is a more competent and effective leader. Things, people, and circumstances are interacted within daily life, and boundaries keep them from having too much interference in decision-making.

It would be very unusual for anyone less than twenty-five years of age to develop to this stage, as the brain is not fully developed until around then. Adults at this stage are free from the world's influences taking over their lives. Relationships with others are enduring and have deepened. The individual is able to interact with people, be in difficult circumstances, and maintain a personally consistent self.

Christians at this stage are seen as mature Christians who are at peace internally while dealing with people who may be immature. They can teach from Scripture the truths of how to live a more Christ-like life. As leaders, Stage Six individuals lead with compassion, empathy, and a listening ear to others' needs and wants. They are not easily offended by someone who may have a differing opinion or thought. The group they are leading can have greater group cohesiveness and will work well together. The Stage Six leader is well respected and sometimes admired by others and will not allow these beliefs to change who they are becoming in Christ.

Stage Six Characteristics

1. The individual in Stage Six has consistency in life, even in difficult situations.
2. They are emotionally peaceful and content and can express anger, anxiety, and sadness where appropriate without losing control.
3. The individual listens to others and can work on understanding their intent, not just their words.
4. The individual can be respectful of self and others over differences without getting prideful or resentful.
5. When asked who they are, Stage Six individuals can express in depth both their positive and negative characteristics while displaying a good self-esteem and self-values.
6. The individual understands people at different levels of development and does not judge or ridicule them.
7. The individual's resources are managed wisely with the awareness that they do not determine his personal significance.
8. The individual is seen as loving, as well as caring, and can establish healthy boundaries.
9. The individual is aware of the continuation of development as a lifelong process and strives not to become complacent.

10. Even when the individual has understanding of Scripture and of people, she continues to desire to learn and grow to a higher level of understanding and depth.

11. The individual has developed a true in-depth empathy so that others' differences are understood and acknowledged.

In the mid-1960's Bev and I attended a small community church where the pastor displayed a maturity level that I had never seen before. He had integrity and understood the Word of God at the deepest level. He could relate to others both seriously and playfully. He related well to people at any stage of development with purpose and caring from the heart and desired them to grow in Christ.

He developed a relationship with a motorcycle club even knowing some of its members were in a local criminal gang. One Sunday he rode his motorcycle and invited them to church. Nine-tenths of the church parking lot was filled with motorcycles. The club came to the service to hear him speak about how God could change their lives. He had quite the relationship with them.

He could interact with children and often did his ape impression as part of the children's sermon. The children loved him. Before coming to our church, he had been a college professor at a well-known theological seminary. I realize now that he had matured to Stage Six and possibly early Stage Seven development. I was wondering the other day, who taught him about maturity and development? He has long since passed away, and from heaven I would really like to hear from him how he was able to find his identity in Christ. I believe he would say that through Scripture and continually seeking God's will, he became the man God had planned for him to be!

Stage Seven Development

Stage Seven Development is characterized by integrations of relativity, movement, and change. This stage is rarely reached in our society today and possibly will never be reached on earth. The individual might be seen as strange or unusual from others' point of view. He is able to see a variety of ways of perceiving and integrating life's experiences and to be aware that a single choice is not the only answer. There is a deep awareness of the meaning and purpose of life.

Christians who reach the early aspects of this stage are seen as striving to be Christ-like. Scripture is read and expressed in a deeper meaning. They care about people and things as part of God's world and can see God's plan in their lives and interact with others accordingly. As leaders, Stage Seven individuals are genuinely caring for others and can facilitate the group's plans and purposes. They value others' opinions and are able to disagree constructively rather than destructively. The Stage Seven leader spends time daily in God's word and is consistently seeking God's will for their life.

Stage Seven Characteristics

1. The individual has inner peace and an outward expression of confidence in God and God's plan for his life.
2. The individual wisely integrates the different influences in life, while making wise choices in what to do.
3. The individual's relationship with others is based on the love of God and discernment of the characteristics of the other person.

4. The Bible is the source of understanding of the deeper meanings in life and a toolbox of alternatives to cope with and manage life.
5. Material things, possessions, and resources are humbly managed with the awareness that all belong to God and are gifts from Him.
6. Difficult circumstances are seen as God-given ways for growth.
7. The individual integrates and manages emotions with thoughtfulness, even in expressions.

We realize this is a lot of information to assimilate all at one time, especially if you are unfamiliar with the developmental process. Take a breath, relax, and allow God to show you the pieces He wants you to focus on right now. Other pieces will come as you are ready for them, and God will continue to direct you in the process of maturity in Christ.

EMOTIONAL INTERPERSONAL MATURITY DEVELOPMENT

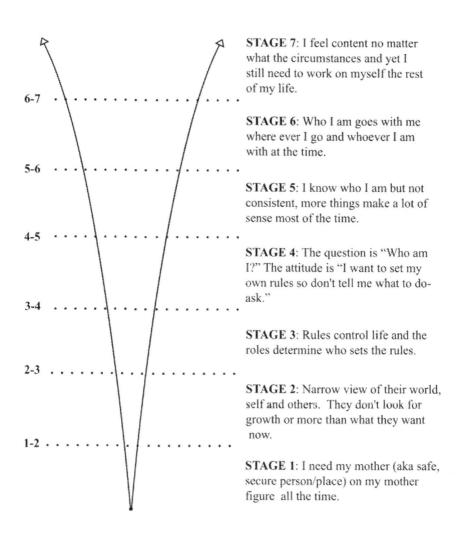

STAGE 7: I feel content no matter what the circumstances and yet I still need to work on myself the rest of my life.

STAGE 6: Who I am goes with me where ever I go and whoever I am with at the time.

STAGE 5: I know who I am but not consistent, more things make a lot of sense most of the time.

STAGE 4: The question is "Who am I?" The attitude is "I want to set my own rules so don't tell me what to do- ask."

STAGE 3: Rules control life and the roles determine who sets the rules.

STAGE 2: Narrow view of their world, self and others. They don't look for growth or more than what they want now.

STAGE 1: I need my mother (aka safe, secure person/place) on my mother figure all the time.

6-7
5-6
4-5
3-4
2-3
1-2

Summary of Stages of Development and Their Characteristics

Stage One and Two:	*Level of Development:* Relatively Undeveloped Lacks a developed self-observer, other-person perspective, and struggles with consequential thinking and alternative thinking. *Controlled by:* Virtually no control Controlled by emotions, other people and things.
Stage Three:	*Level of Development:* Minimal self-observer, other-person perspective, consequential thinking, and alternative thinking. *Controlled by:* Some control Controlled by emotions, thoughts, others, relationships, pride, past and future and things.
Stage Four:	*Level of Development:* Mostly Present Begins to develop a much stronger capacity for self-observation, other-person perspective, consequential thinking and alternative thinking. *Controlled by:* Growing capacity for free choice Dominated by pride, guilt, other people, physical body, past, present, and future concerns.
Stage Five:	*Level Of Development:* Stronger and increasing capacity for self-observation, other-person perspective, consequential and alternative thinking. Is increasingly able to use SOCA in dealing with life experiences. Has a better internal boundary system to deal with the outside world.

Controlled by: less controlled by and more actively choosing. Increasing self-awareness is lessening the domination and control by internal and external distractors. Individual is less likely to be dominated and unwittingly lead by impulses and more free to make choices in the resources of time, money, and affection.

Stage Six *Level of Development:* Strongly Present
Development of SOCA is a consistent part of life and boundaries are strong. SOCA skills enable proficiency with issues in life. Belief system is clearly established. Is active in living out this belief system by striving to be committed and surrendered to a Christ-like life.

Controlled by: Choices consistent with values
Individual exhibits autonomy from influences of the natural world and impulses in making choices. They are aware of consistently moderating impulses into alignment with what they value. Life is congruent and authentic.

HELIX OF DEVELOPMENT

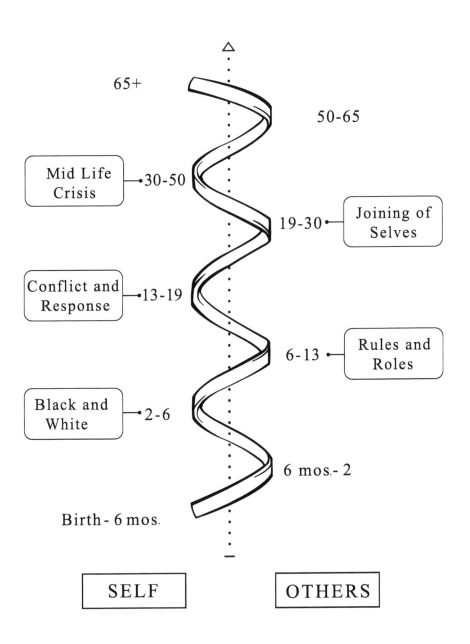

65+

50-65

Mid Life
Crisis — 30-50

19-30 — Joining of
Selves

Conflict and
Response — 13-19

6-13 — Rules and
Roles

Black and
White — 2-6

6 mos.- 2

Birth - 6 mos.

SELF

OTHERS

CHAPTER 7

WHAT IS SPIRITUAL DISCIPLINE?

The chapters that follow are foundations for spiritual discipline. One definition of discipline is training in moral development. What encourages, motivates, or provides energy for discipline? I believe it is the love of Christ (see Ephesians 3:17–19) The love of God surpasses knowledge and strengthens us inwardly for discipline. Without discipline, we fall backward in our spiritual maturity. We begin to live in the flesh and the world.

How many of you have read *Finishing Strong* by Steve Farrar? Have you heard of Chuck Templeton or Byron Clifford? In 1945–1946 they were seen as the most gifted and possibly the most powerful preachers the church had seen in centuries. People lined up to hear them preach. Just five years later, Templeton left the ministry to pursue a career in radio and television. He had decided he was no longer a believer in Christ. I believe he was probably at Stage Three development, and when he began Stage Four he did as many teens do: he decided, "This is not me." Pride, things of the world, and other people's influence distracted his thoughts and feelings, and as a result he lost his true self, which was in Christ.

By 1954, Byron Clifford had lost his family, his ministry, his health, and his life. He died of cirrhosis of the liver. He too had not developed maturity beyond Stage Three or Stage Four. Clearly, neither of these men was able to be self-observant with the Holy Spirit's direction to continue to grow their faith in Christ.

What about the third man who started with Templeton and Clifford? The third man was Billy Graham, who continues to show growth and maturity with humility and understanding of God's Word. Is that true of other men who have entered the ministry? Farrar wrote about John Bisagno and how he kept track of twenty-four of his peers, most in their twenties, who had given themselves to the Lord. By the time Bisagno was fifty-three years old, only three of the twenty-four remained faithful to their commitment to the Lord. Did the other twenty-one get to Stage Four and declare, "This is not for me?"

Farrar also wrote about Howard Hendricks's study of 246 men in full-time ministry who experienced personal and moral failure. Roughly ten each month for two years failed in their ministry. Howard Hendricks said, in the Christian life that it is not how we start that matters, but how you finish for the Lord that is important.

It is far too easy for doubts, feelings of disappointments from the past, or worries about the future to distract us from growing in spiritual maturity. And yet when we are working toward maturity in Christ, we strangely find ourselves at peace and content with ourselves and others. Even in difficult times, we can rejoice in what the Lord is bringing to our lives through His grace.

Again, with tears of humility I thank God that He has helped me sustain growth, even in life's trials and temptations.

The Meaning of the Word *Self*

The self is an ancient concept and appears in most European languages. The root meaning of *self* is "likeness or sameness." Additionally, "likeness and sameness" is also the meaning of the word *image*. In Genesis 1:26, God says, "Let Us make man in Our image, according to our likeness," and in Genesis 1:27, "God created man in His own image, in the image of God He created him; male and female He created them" (NASB).

Image and *likeness* do not mean "equality." Many people and many churches have a very negative view of the word *self,* interpreting it more as selfish, not a choice of which image to emulate: God or the world. In other words, are you choosing to be an image of God or the world? Today many churches would like to leave the word *self* at the door; the problem is, that leaves us with nothing to love God. It is with our whole "self" that we love, serve, and worship Him. If we fail to love with our growing and mature "self," what will we love God with?

At the heart of this discussion are two systems, with divergent views on self and love. One system is based on accepting love and the other on earning love. One view will steer the ship of self onto the rocks and the other to open possibilities. Scripture says in Genesis 2:16-17, "And the Lord God commanded the man, 'You are free to eat from any tree in the garden; but you must not eat from the tree of the knowledge of good and evil, for when you eat of it you will surely die.'" In chapter 3 the man and woman ate from the tree of knowledge of good and evil and at that point they became self-aware of good and evil; then when they saw each other naked, they felt guilt and fear and told God "I was afraid because I was naked, so I hid myself" (see Genesis 3:10). Even early, we wanted to blame something or someone for our actions and feelings.

When we broke the image of God by disobedience, we then took on the image (likeness) of things in the world, including our own thoughts and feelings, images of other people, and other things. Through the work of the Holy Spirit, we can take on the likeness or image of Christ (Romans 8:29). Further, from Galatians 5:16–26, we can be in the likeness of the flesh and what that looks like, or the likeness (image) of the Spirit and what that looks like.

The dictionary has over 500 words with *self* as a prefix, from *self-abandonment* to *self-worship*. One of the meanings is "being of the same substance." The word *selfish* is interesting as the *-ish* means "having the bad qualities of or belonging to."

The "Bad Me" Image

If you grew up in a church like mine, then you'd understand why I wince when the topic of self comes up. It's kind of the summation and source of everything wrong with the world and especially "me." Countless times I wished to be freed from this bad, bad self and to be something else. Not really sure what that something else was, but I longed for some distance from the badness I was certain "God said" resided there.

This client's story has been echoed hundreds of times throughout the years of my practice, and I have given considerable thought to the circumstances that lead to these kinds of personal perspectives. This common view of what the Bible or church says actually reflects a particular or a selective truth about sin, love, grace, and forgiveness.

That's why my own experience was so different from the "bad me" self-image portrayed above, and what was that difference? My mother. She went to heaven to teach the angels how to love. Because of her, I knew the love of Christ even as a child. This love was a protective covering, a balancing of grace, against the judgment that many Christians feel. This foundation of love provided a secure sanctuary, enabling me to view "self" more objectively. I was well positioned to experience growth, and although I often had feelings of inadequacy, there was no guilt or shame.

I believe it is what we believe in—the sustaining grace of God or the foolishness of the world—that determines the difference. We need to strive to be the self that God has ordained us to be. God allowed His Son to come to minister to and die for our "self." The choice is ours, and we can work on developing maturity as we develop ourselves and allow the Holy Spirit to mold us into the image that God wants for us. This is an ongoing process that can be filled with joy, peace, and comfort such as only God can give.

There will forever be a battle in the world, a battle declaring what is good and evil, a battle seeking to devour those who are not well rooted in the Lord. God gave us a free will, and like it or not, that puts you in charge of deciding which you will serve: good or evil; God or

Satan; God's kingdom or the world. How can you fight such a battle without a self that is fortified with the armor of God? You cannot; you will fail and be devoured. Caution on this lifetime journey we travel: choose God or choose death.

Built for reflection and relationship, mankind's search has become an endless quest to fill this inner void. To look at something and to become like it is a reflection. Materialism is a popular American approach to this "self"-help dilemma. Our lives are filled with and reflect the things we own, things that will not bring meaning. So we "do." We build, we buy, and we accomplish tasks, but in the end, we can acquire a world of things and not have a mature self. Things or accomplishments, awards or honors do not form the self, nor will the self be mature in the image of these worldly things. The self is what God has begun in us; it is the heart, soul, and body God entrusted to us. Do you want to reflect from the heart and soul the gifts and talents God has given you? I am sure you want to.

Many people come to Christ and bring all their previous views of self with them. Because they have valued things, they now get things for God; because they found meaning in doing and being busy, they now do and are busy for God. The trouble with this perspective is that it doesn't really meet our deepest personal longings, and instead of reflecting God, our lives are really reflecting a God made in our image, not His. It just doesn't work, because that isn't God's design. It is no wonder that many are frustrated in their Christian experience and are leaving the church in droves. The good news is that God has made a better way in Christ.

From the therapist's chair:

> When I was a "green" therapist, I was a little
> intimidated by the pastor or elder sitting across from
> me, pouring out their hearts that God had abandoned
> them. Depressed and uncertain of their future, many
> had given up on their life's goals of following God
> wherever. I began to see a pattern, a pattern that at
> first scared me, yet I decided to risk and began to
> share what my picture of God looked like with these
> clients.
>
> I have a childlike belief that God created me in His
> image for a reason, a purpose only He could have
> designed. I began to share with these individuals that
> their self was created in His image and that they were
> not forgotten. On the contrary, God wanted them to
> develop and mature into a Christ likeness. As they
> began to understand that their self was a reflection, a
> mirror, or an image of God; they began to understand
> how they had allowed the worldly perspective of
> "self" to control who they thought they should be.
> Eventually, they began to allow God to create in them
> a concept of "self" that could grow and mature and
> withstand the trials of this world.

His plan is not that we clean ourselves up and then shine, but that
Christ shines His hope through our brokenness and shows the world
a way out of despair, with authenticity and without hypocrisy.

The self is not an obstacle to Christlikeness that needs to be destroyed as is taught and implied by some in the church. It is the mirror that reflects Christ to the world. Reaching the highest level of personal growth, self-consistency, occurs when we are reflecting God. In this reflection there is surrender and trust, which paradoxically results in finding more of the self our heart has always desired. Christ likeness then is not the obliteration, minimization or in any way diminishment of the self, being Christ like is the greatest fulfillment of what the self was created to be.

Self Means Likeness or Reflection; Whom Do You Want to Reflect?

"For you created my inmost being, you knit me together in my mother's womb. I praise you because I am fearfully and wonderfully made; your works are wonderful, I know that full well" (Psalm 139:13–14).

The 80/20 Principle

The 80/20 principle helps us understand how and why we see and interpret things the way we do. Many internal factors influence our perceptions and interpretations. Two strong factors are the level of our maturity and the strength of our boundaries. The less mature we are, the more we will see and hear things personally and emotionally. As we develop in maturity, we become more objective and less personal in our interpretations. As we continue in development, we are able to deal with difficult circumstances or people and maintain an internal peace for the outcome, even in sorrow when it is not positive. "I feel sorry for how it turned out, but I am okay."

Let me define the principle for you. The 80 percent is what is in our heart; the 20 percent is what is from the outside. So the 80 percent is inside each one of us, while the 20 percent is in and of the world. What is in our heart determines how we deal with what comes in from the outside world. We read in Mark 7:14–16 these words of Jesus to the crowd: "Listen to me, everyone, and understand this, Nothing outside a man can make him 'unclean' by going into him. Rather, it is what comes out of a man that makes him 'unclean'." In verses 18–19, Jesus explains to His disciples, "Are you so dull? ... Don't you see that nothing that enters a man from the outside can make him "unclean'? For it doesn't go into his heart but into his stomach, and then out of his body." In verses 20–23, He continues, "What comes out of a man is what makes him 'unclean'. For from within, out of men's hearts, come evil thoughts, sexual immorality, theft, murder, adultery, greed, malice, deceit, lewdness, envy, slander, arrogance and folly. All these evils come from inside and make a man 'unclean'."

So much for blaming others for your words or actions! It is easy to blame the outside for what we do, but even in the worst of circumstances, as when I was in Africa, I have seen how the inside full of the joy of the Lord determines how an individual will experience life and how the individual will manage outside circumstances. Immature Christians have not developed and are still like children, for whom all of these things are still in control and determine how the outside is perceived and what they do in response.

OUR WORLD VIEW

How do we view; perceive; understand; process life?!

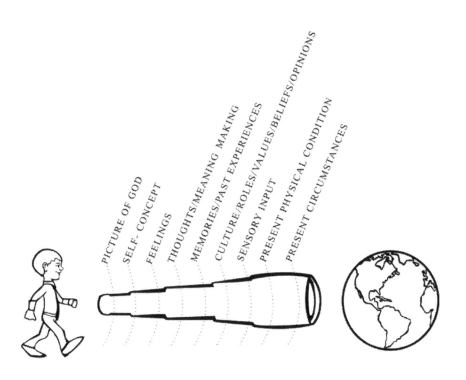

Our Worldview

From the therapist's chair: At some point during my practice, I needed to explain to survivors in clear and concise words that how they were viewing the world probably was not the reality. Trauma survivors often develop a worldview that is not accurate because of what they believe about themselves and what they believe about the world and their place in their world. The diagram above is what I drew out one day. Let me explain:

Think about looking out at your world through a large camera, one with the capacity to insert many lenses into it. Some of those lenses might be:

1. The first and most important lens is our picture of God: how do we see God? (as gentle and loving or angry and judging).
2. Our self-concept is the next lens in the view: how do we see ourselves? (as smart, worthy, and lovable or stupid, miserable, and unwanted).
3. The next lens represents our feelings: how and what are we feeling right now? (for example, depressed, angry, happy, or content).
4. How about our thoughts about what we are seeing? Are we able to find meaning within our view of the outside world?
5. Our culture is our next lens. What are the roles, values, beliefs, and opinions we observe about the outside culture where we live?
6. Sensory input: What are my eyes seeing? What am I tasting or smelling? Am I too hot or too cold?

7. Present physical condition: Am I tired or exhausted, hungry or satisfied, or in pain?

8. Present circumstances: What is happening in this moment that is influencing my perception and understanding of the outside world?

Now consider all the things that might be placed between these lenses that cloud or dirty up our view of the world. These interferences might have been of our own creation, or others might have instilled these interferences. I have made a list below for you to consider.

Factors in the 80/20 Perspective

Of our perspective, 80 percent is based on our inside—our heart, our moral standards, our authenticity, our spiritual teachings and beliefs—not what is happening on the outside around us. So how is it we give away some of the 80 percent? (Some individuals give away all the 80 percent.) Here are some factors I believe can affect our perspective. Think of it as looking through distorted glasses at our ability to perceive things. It is how things fit together. It becomes our explanation of our experiences. I have compiled a list of eleven factors that might have direct or indirect influences on our perspective of the world and thus influence the workings of the 80/20 principle. These factors can cloud or dirty up our lenses to view our world.

1. Age and physical condition: pain, tiredness, sickness, lack of sleep, quality of the senses (sight and hearing), gender, or physical challenges.

2. Stress levels: the demands on our attention, and our perceived expectations of others.

3. History: loved, abused, over-controlled, lack of structure, disciplined, consistent or inconsistent, parents divorced or together, only child, birth order, adoption or fostered.

4. Emotional: anxious, angry, depressed, resentful, cautious, hyper vigilant, peaceful, confident, from highly sensitive to alexithymia (total lack of emotional awareness), happy, or encouraged.

5. PTSD: military experience, traumatic experiences, survivor or victim.

6. Cultural: where you were raised in the world, ethnic background, amount of moving around during childhood or as an adult, city, urban, rural, language spoken in the home.

7. Spiritual: relationship with God, atheist, Scientology, disinterested or unbelief, lack of hope and fatalistic viewpoint.

8. Intelligence: highly intelligent to very bright, open-minded, closed-minded, open to new perspectives or unable to change, intelligent with common sense, or unable to manage daily life structure.

9. Financial experience: wealthy, upper middle class, lower middle class, in poverty, overindulged, underprivileged, encouraged with allowances, work experience, successes in attempts to work.

10. Educational opportunities: finished high school, community college or trade school, university experience or degrees, postgrad work and experiences, opportunities for education aboard. Life experience or street smarts.

11. Employment opportunities: success in securing gainful employment, long-term employment with same company, layoffs and restarts, business owner or employee.

To clarify further, if we are viewing the present through the distortion of the past, how will our perspective be influenced? If we were labeled and made to feel stupid or helpless all our life, what type of worldview will we have? Sometimes we are not aware of the filters that influence us and how we see things or how the patterns develop.

I know for myself there was a huge interference in my self-concept that I was not aware of until my midtwenties, when I began to have children. I know that I wanted to read to my children, and I wanted them to enjoy stories as a bonding time. In my view of my world, somewhere locked away between my self-concept and my feelings was a fear so huge I was not sure I could face it. You see, I could not read; yes, you read that correctly. Somehow, as I was going to school in the late 1940s, reading and possibly any other subject was not of importance because the primary goal was babysitting while the parents worked in the shipyards building warships. Besides, the second-grade teacher told me I would never amount to anything, and I believed her.

Anyway, the bottom line is I couldn't read and was about to have my first child. So I confronted myself and decided, "Yes, you can." I began that very day in the Richmond Public Library in the children's section with the simplest book I could find, progressing through the rows of books until one day I entered the adult library. What a process that was, and what I learned about myself along the way.

I chose not to let the outside harsh words define the 80 percent of my inside. I chose not to allow the outside world steal from me my 80 percent. I chose to confront the filters that were keeping me stuck and forge forward to a healthier, mature self.

How often do you hear your spouse say something, and you intensely react to his or her words without thinking about your filter and lenses? I had a forty-year-old male and his wife in the office, and right there he heard something his wife said, stood up on his feet, and yelled at her. He was reacting from about 95 percent of his negative and critical internal state. After I directed him to sit, I told him he was reacting to the words his parents had said to him as a child and how these words caused stress and embarrassment to him, even as a child, not what his wife had just said. He missed his wife's intent completely. How often do you give your 80 percent inside away so that you may only have 20 percent left to cope with the outside world?

Find an empty paper towel tube, and imagine that as you look through it there are your own individual filters that you can lower, depending on your inner state that day. Now look through the tube, and imagine how you are seeing a particular situation or person with the addition of the anxious filter, the angry filter, or maybe the past experience filter. Write your thoughts down. Now imagine a different filter for the same situation. How would a joyful, unconditionally loving, or healthy filter change the outcome? Write this down, and decide how you want to view your world. What filters influence you the most, and which ones need to change permanently?

Keep in mind that if we maintain a healthy, growing and maturing self-observer, then we are able to be aware of the factors that influence our perceptions. We can never be 100 percent objective in how we view things, but it's important to be aware of what these influences are (feelings, past, people, culture, etc.) and how much they might interfere with our perception.

Recently, I had a conversation with a client from the Japanese culture about how her cultural background influences how she is perceived by others and how she perceives her circumstances. The conversation helped me recognize again that I need to take cultural differences into perspective even in different areas of our United States.

Mark's Story

Mark was a freshman from a small town, and when his family moved, he found himself at a much larger high school. He was a Christian and attended a small church where he felt comfortable being himself. He had difficulty fitting into the new high school and soon found himself being bullied by older students. He found himself feeling suicidal and just was about to give up.

Mark went to his youth director, who suggested he talk to me about the situation. Early in our sessions, Mark understood the principles developed in SOCA and almost immediately started applying them at home. When we went deeper into the 80/20 principle, he really understood what was happening at school. You see, he realized that very little of the bullying situation was about him, and a full 80 percent or more was about the kids who were bullying him. He was able to stand up for himself, face to face with the bullies, and tell them exactly what he had learned.

He and another student who was experiencing the same bullying from the same kids decided to go to the administration to talk about the problem. The bullies were required to do some community service and outreach classes on respect for others. Mark is really glad he learned about SOCA and the 80/20 principle from a biblical perspective.

From Bev: "I clearly remember a similar situation with one of our own children. The situation was about feelings between junior high girls. When I sat down as a mom and explained that possibly all the anger coming from the other girl was about the other girl and not about what my daughter believed it to be (herself, my daughter), then she understood that many times what we see is not what is really happening. She was able to sit down with the other girl and talk things out. They were never really close friends, but at least the tension decreased, and we could move forward."

When looking through your world filters, how often do you believe a distorted picture? Do you become guilty or feel ashamed because you believe it is your fault? What if you look again with the eyes of Christ at the same situation? Stop assuming that it's about you, and know it is probably more about the other person.

We are experiencing such an increase in similar situations that Mark was caught in throughout middle schools and high schools in this country. We need to instill in our kids and grandkids that what others are saying is only 20 percent about what is happening outside them; it's 80 percent about the person saying it. So why does it hurt so badly that many young people are attempting and committing suicide? They are giving away the other 40, 60, or even 90 percent of themselves. It's not that others are taking it; they are giving it away.

One of the statements I make to young people often is *"Whose life is this, and how do you want to live it?"*

I read a book years ago entitled *Stand Up for Yourself*, in which the author was embarrassed in a very public setting and refused to continue in the competition. That refusal played out in his life until he was a young adult, when he began to realize, "Wait, I do not have to allow others to define who I am, I can define myself!" So how do you allow others to define you? Do you keep the things of the world separate and not allow them to take so much of you, or are you giving yourself away daily? What's happened today? Can you say you have stood in integrity about your beliefs?

Now that you are beginning to understand how outside influences can have a major impact on you, you need to realize this process happens to everyone. If someone is yelling at you, it is 80 percent or more about that person, not you. This is where other-person perspective comes in. When other people are inwardly at peace, then you will see them treat others with thoughtful concern. The inside determines what we do with the outside.

CHAPTER 8

UNDERSTANDING THE HOLY SPIRIT AS GUIDE, PROTECTOR, AND HELPER

Are you ready to put on the armor of God and fight through to change and grow? Ephesians 6:10–18, the great passage on this subject, begins, "Put on the whole armor of God." Before leaving the house we usually make sure we are fully dressed—shirt, pants, and even shoes. Usually our hair is combed and makeup applied. Yet how often do we leave the safety of home without being fully clothed in the armor of God?

Our heavenly Father, Jesus Christ, and the Holy Spirit are stronger than anything Satan can conjure up to entangle us and lay us low. Without being fully prepared, how do we expect to defend ourselves when Satan does shoot those arrows at us? Life is hard, sometimes very hard, and we need to be prepared. Satan wants nothing less than to confuse us into believing the lies of the world and to keep us stuck in old patterns of behavior. Are you ready to put on the armor and fight to change? We encourage you to continue in the process, at your own pace; take breaks when needed, and forge ahead as you can. We are praying you will continue growing and maturing in Christ.

As a beginning psychologist, I would use the Stages of Development during sessions and have greatly refined and expanded these as I understood more and more about human behavior. Therapeutic tools such as SOCA were developed over time. Other tools also developed, and the following is one of them.

From the therapist's chair: The Holy Spirit was at work in both Bev and me, showing us how to develop a clear and concise way to share how the daily areas of our lives can either shape or interfere with our growth process. One day, we both came into the office hallway with a circle we had drawn during a client session and were amazed at the similarities in both of our drawings. Mine had the word *self* in the middle and the areas of emotions, past, present, and future; Bev's had the self in the middle and other people, emotions, and thoughts encircling the self. As we expanded these diagrams, I was sharing with a group of students at Multnomah Bible College. One of them said, "Why don't you put the Holy Spirit in the center with the self?" and the very same week one of the pastors that Bev was sharing with said he thought the Holy Spirit should be in the center with the self. Thus grew the formation of three diagrams we have used for many years. We have described the three diagrams in many ways, and I think since we are writing about this, we need to create a visual picture for you as an explanation.

Imagine for just a moment an egg without a shell. Without this protective shell, the delicate life could never form within the now shapeless blob, and every outside force could easily penetrate. Emotionally we are like that egg without a shell from our birth and throughout our development. The self lacks structure and is seeking a form, and every outside force easily penetrates, disrupting the formation of this oh so delicate living and breathing being. When people yield their life to God, the Holy Spirit brings a bold offering and opportunity that is something like that protective shell. Unlike the shell offered by the mother hen, this shell truly begins with the acceptance of Jesus Christ and is complete only at the point of entering heaven. The first diagram depicts a non-Christian, and there is no internal covering or protection from the Holy Spirit.

Entanglement
Non-Christian

Diagram #1 represents the non-Christian. Such individuals may or may not have knowledge of God's grace through Jesus Christ but have not accepted Jesus as their personal Savior. All ten aspects (thoughts, feelings, other people, things, job, etc.) that are part of their life experience are allowed to take over who they are and how they react to life.

Feelings, things, pride, or the past are like arrows being shot at the very core of the individual. Without the Holy Spirit to direct and instruct them on life's journey, these arrows (past, feelings, thoughts, their own body, or other people) penetrate their core, causing fear, anxiety, depression, and confusion on how to control and form their self in life. Not only do they grasp at whatever seems to strike their interest by "doing whatever seems right in their own eyes," they wander about like sheep without a Shepherd, oppressed by life, struggling to form a self without the Holy Spirit.

Imagine striving every day to be all that you believe is necessary to be "happy" yet never finding contentment, fulfillment, or enjoyment. Thus is life without the grace of Christ's sacrifice and redemption and the guidance and companionship of the Holy Spirit! The self, located at the center of the diagram, is prey to all of life's areas, and the world's arrows will penetrate inside the interior circle with pain and confusion. Stop at diagram #1 and ask yourself, "Every day how many arrows representing my different areas of life are penetrating my self and leaving me in pain, with hopelessness and a never-ending struggle to redefine myself each day?" That is a heavy question? Let's continue to find some relief.

ENTANGLEMENT

Non-Christian

Messy Boundaries

Diagram #2 represents individuals who believe in God and have accepted Jesus Christ as personal Savior. The Holy Spirit is present with them, yet they allow distractions in the areas of their life to interfere with their relationship with God. The self is still placed over God, and even though the Holy Spirit is present, there are gaps in their covering and protection where the arrows of life can still get through. There is lacking a consistent partnership of the self, God, and the Holy Spirit.

Such individuals are vulnerable to being swept up into the struggle of their feelings, things, job, pride, or interactions with others. They might ask the Holy Spirit to help in some areas, and when the Holy Spirit does provide the solution, they may stop short of following through or even rebel against what the Holy Spirit has spoken to them. The world's arrows do not penetrate as far into their inner self, and life certainly has more structure and meaning, and yet they are still struggling with many areas of life. How often do you find yourself striving hard to follow God and partner with the Holy Spirit, yet when life happens, you become discouraged, depressed, and ready to give up?

God's desire is for each one of us to be fully clothed in Christ, and He offers the Holy Spirit as our protection, promising to be consistently there every day during our growth process. Unfortunately, I have met many Christians who are stuck in the messy boundaries of diagram #2. They have believed and accepted Christ yet struggle with the growth God desires for them in daily areas of their life. We are going to discuss in depth each of these areas later in this chapter, so keep reading and growing. Write down the life areas that are piercing through to the self, and begin to pray over how these areas might change and grow.

MESSY BOUNDARIES

Individual believes in God and the Holy Spirit, yet

Allows distractions that interfere with relationship

With God

Healthy Boundaries

Life is going to happen every day, and in diagram #3 all ten of the life areas will happen daily. Individuals with a firm and solid foundation, with the Holy Spirit as protection and helper, have God in the center of their life. Their self is consistently in a growing relationship with God and the Holy Spirit. Yes, life's influences are still there, but with God in control, they can breathe easy in His plan for their life.

As the Holy Spirit becomes more influential, the arrows are stopped as we listen and follow the Holy Spirit's wisdom and instruction. At Stage Five and Stage Six the Christian individual maintains healthy boundaries against the things in the world and is yielded and enfolded by the Holy Spirit. Diagram #3 represents such individuals with solid lines between the world influences, the Holy Spirit, and the self. Those described in diagram #3 consider feelings, job, other people, and a host of life's complexities, and then commit to a whole new way— through the eyes of the Holy Spirit rather than only through their own interpretations. The Holy Spirit's wisdom and protection have provided the protection for the delicate life to fully form and emerge, growing and ready for life's struggles. With God's presence, there is a peace and contentment that we can only find in consistency with God.

Many of us have enjoyed the Trees of Mystery in Northern California. One of the amazing or perhaps mysterious things about these giant redwoods is that they are still growing. As they come closer and closer to full maturity, the growth does slow down, but it never ever stops. Christians are like these trees; never stop growing. There are still things to change and refine, ways of doing life differently, and the exciting part of life is learning how the Holy Spirit is directing us to continually grow.

HEALTHY BOUNDARIES

(Balance - All life's influences are still there,
but are not in control. God is in control)

From Bev:

> I accepted Jesus as my personal Savior as a child, as
> any good Baptist girl would do in the early 1950s.
> I attended youth group faithfully, partially to have
> something to do and to see my friends. I would listen
> and even cry at the appropriate times when my friends
> were crying; but it was not until I moved to Merced
> that God's plan became clearer. As a volunteer youth
> coordinator I found myself studying Scripture in
> preparation for youth Bible study and retreats. I
> began to realize I only had a superficial relationship
> with Jesus and was not listening too well to the Holy
> Spirit. My faith was very childlike, and I did not fully
> understand the role of the Holy Spirit in my life.
>
> I began to read other books by authors like A. W.
> Tozer, Charles Spurgeon, and many others. I studied
> the character of God, slowly realizing I needed to
> grow up. I desired to learn "Who am I?" in Christ
> and strived to become the woman God intended me to
> be. Through many tears and loss; joy and celebration
> I now have a stronger concept of who I am in Christ.
> I will be seventy this year, and I pray daily that I will
> continue to grow and develop into the woman God
> desires for me. Ironically, I am asked often by young
> mothers whom I have the privilege of mentoring, "I
> don't know who I am in Christ," or "How do I find
> my true self in Christ?" Those are two of the greatest
> questions for me to respond to.

From Steve: "God is really in the center of my life. When I am yielded and united with Christ in mind and heart, it is possible to maintain balance even when my past comes barreling back into my present, even when individuals in my life are creating chaos; even if I lose my job or a loved one. For, I am more than a conqueror through Christ Jesus. The tender and fragile life that is found by Christ and takes root in Him can experience a towering destiny."

Journaling and Reflection

1. Take time and consider which of these diagrams best describes where you find yourself today.

2. Have you ever thought about how important and necessary it is to keep the Holy Spirit in the center and foremost in your life as a Christian?

3. What skill will you need to develop with the Lord's help to keep the Holy Spirit in the center?

4. Remember, the word *self* means "sameness," "likeness," or reflection." When the Holy Spirit is not in the center of our lives, they take on the likeness of things, so that instead of reflecting Christ, we reflect "things" or our emotions such as anger or jealousy.

   a. Think back; can you recall a time or times when your life was reflecting what other people wanted from you? If so, how did you respond?

   b. Can you think of times when your life reflected your unmanaged emotions? If so, what were those emotions?

   c. Can you think of a time when you were reflecting the Holy Spirit well in your life? Describe the experience in detail.

5. As you reflect on your growth now, describe the times of discovery where you gained more insight into your own thinking.

6. Are you able to find an area or areas that are hindering your growth?

    a. List them.

    b. Ask God for His help for growth in each of these areas you have identified.

    c. Commit to pray daily about each area, and watch how God changes these areas of interference with your growth.

CHAPTER 9

WHAT INTERFERES WITH DEVELOPMENT?

What interferes with your development? We need to explore ten of the most common interferences to growth so that you might have a framework to build strong barriers in partnership with the Holy Spirit to deflect these arrows. All of us, male and female, need to be heard, understood, and cared for from birth till death. It is my desire that you listen to yourself while discovering which interferences you struggle with and how you might change them.

Introduction to Feelings

Sometimes clients look at their therapists as placid pools of knowledge, never ruffled, emotionally flat lines. Nothing could be farther from the truth. I am a part of many dynamic, meaningful relationships and working continually on my own growth. I am aware of and wrestling with some of my own development, and the lessons I teach, I need to practice daily myself. There is a unique relationship with God, with myself, and with clients that continuously builds on these principles of growth.

Of all the barriers to growth, none has a more prominent place than our emotions. As I often say during counseling sessions, nothing separates couples, or for that matter any individuals in relationship, more than unresolved emotions. Although this is simply said, it is not simply practiced! We all feel the gravitational pull to be caught up in our emotional roller coasters or someone else's emotional experience.

Feelings are a tricky subject to tackle because they are both necessary and also an opportunity to be overwhelmed and completely carried away. The perspectives on how to constructively benefit from our emotions span the gamut from completely disregarding feelings on one end of the continuum to the other end where what I feel at the moment rules my every move.

The value of emotions can best be seen where they are completely absent. A medical condition, alexithymia describes this total lack of emotional awareness. I worked with a client with this diagnosis, whose interpersonal relationships were a complete disaster. On the other hand, the prominence of emotions forms an intense roller-coaster ride, which is a strong interference in spiritual growth. Remember Bev's experience with the car's sun visor? She will admit the intense emotional trauma present in her daily life heightened by the onset of premenopausal episodes, and yet she realized she needed to take responsibility for her feelings.

Our emotions inform us of our preferences. We might say, "What do I feel like doing tonight? Go to the movies and dinner; or stay at home?" Without feelings, there is little differentiation emotionally between options, even between options that are pleasurable. I often say feelings are not right or wrong, good or bad, black or white. (1) They are just the way I feel at the moment, and (2) how I respond or react while experiencing the feeling is what makes the difference: I can be angry without becoming the anger and acting out.

On the other end of the spectrum, some individuals who have a tendency to become their emotions are so completely dialed into their feelings that experiencing them can be a distressing flood, resulting in paralysis to make decisions and to respond rationally.

> Jessica wakes early, lying in bed, earnestly wanting to get up and fix her husband breakfast before he leaves, but as she lies there, she is thinking about what he would want and has a lengthy conversation in her mind about why eggs would be better than oatmeal. Then she gets stuck on sliced orange or apple wedges. He likes apple wedges the most, but she knows that he's fighting a cold, and the oranges have the vitamin C he really needs. But then she's triggered by the thought that he might be angry with her for choosing oranges, because sometimes he accuses her of mothering him, and she certainly doesn't want that this morning. The idea that he might be angry prompts her to hedge the orange wedges with looking extra attractive, so she begins to go through a list of things to do before she appears in the kitchen, and just about that moment she hears the back door close and the car start as her husband heads off to work. She bursts into tears (still in bed). What kind of wife wouldn't get out of bed to fix her husband breakfast after all?—and

> weeping reminds her of her best friend, who is getting
> a divorce, and ...

I cannot count the number of times counseling sessions have begun with such a recounted story, leading the conversation to the feelings experienced during this whole internal dialogue. The extreme paralysis that may occur through emotional flooding, illustrated by Jessica's story, justifies some who actually encourage people to ignore their emotions. These individuals encourage others to live in their head, making decisions based only on what the facts dictate, and their feelings will fall in line. The engine is in the mind, and the feelings dutifully follow as the lowly caboose. Ignoring and stuffing feelings and pretending you don't care about them, when actually your emotions are screaming at you, will complicate your life journey and keep you stuck in the unresolved feelings.

From the therapist's chair: "I have to be honest: one of the most difficult aspects of working with trauma survivors is the buried, stuffed, and often forgotten feelings. Difficult feelings can sometimes be totally unrecognizable, and yet those feelings may drive a person's behavior throughout life, whether consciously or unconsciously. When brave individuals begin the process of facing the not-so-forgotten feelings, therapeutic progress can be made. Individuals who choose to ignore or rebury their unresolved feelings struggle with the recovery process. Feelings have to be resolved to move forward; otherwise, the unresolved feelings have the power over you and your life."

It is important to mention that there is a gender component to emotional perception. Females have much better, stronger, and quicker access to their emotions than do males as a group. The neurological pathways for a female to recognize emotions are much more developed than are the male's pathways. That is not to say males don't have feelings; they do. Males are as capable of recognizing and experiencing feelings as females are; it just might take a male a little longer to figure it all out. Many males are very connected with their feelings, and many females are not, but these are more the exceptions than the rule. To visualize this gender difference, think of females' connections to emotions as fiber optics, while males are on dial-up; while females are taking a four-lane freeway, a male might be on a two-lane road down to a cow path toward recognition of his feelings.

Acknowledging differences is essential to understanding each other and oneself. If you are having difficulty connecting with your emotions, it isn't bad. It's simply your starting point.

As you enter this section on emotions, remember that God gave us feelings. He created feelings, He understands them, and He certainly will be there with you. Feelings are part of "who we are" in Christ; they are useful and have an important, essential place in our lives and our relationship with Him. After all, God displays emotions! It's impossible to read Scripture without seeing God's heart for the things He loves and those He dislikes. He's actually open and honest with His feelings. We are made in His image and reflect Him, and this very much includes these emotional aspects of ourselves as well.

Anxiety and Fear

Imagine for a moment that you are walking in the woods. It's a lovely day, the sun is shining, and then you hear it: a twig snaps loudly in the formerly tranquil forest. It is very close. Add to this that yesterday you read of a cougar alert, and this sound is suddenly brimming with a new, perhaps ominous meaning.

The natural feelings of fear and anxiety can begin to act protectively here to increase awareness of both self and the environment. These feelings might prompt you to pause and look around very carefully, especially in the direction of that snapping sound, and when you see that it was probably caused by a squirrel, you resume your walk, but take a trail that leads to more known open areas. Another response might be to freeze momentarily, head away from the sound, and then blindly run screaming as you go deeper and deeper into the forest. Two very different possibilities, from the same knowledge and sound of a snapping twig; one where fear and anxiety has informed your sensibilities, and the other where fear and anxiety have replaced all rational thought.

From Murl:

> I was rather shy as a teen and young adult. Even playing basketball in front of an audience bothered me, but it was also a part of my small steps forward. I'll never forget agreeing to speak in front of my home church for Youth Sunday. It was an internal struggle to get up in front of all those people; yet I didn't want this fear to stand in the way of doing what I felt God was putting in my heart to say. I was so anxious that I finished within ten minutes (I'd been given half an hour to speak). I learned that facing and moving toward my fears really was making me more free.

The Bible contains over 450 scriptures on anxiety and fear. God has lots to say on this subject and for good reason; there are lots of arrows to dodge in life, perils within and perils outside. There are many things that a healthy, informed fear helps us avoid that are terribly destructive, but anxiety can also block us from being all that God wants us to be. Our fear and anxiety need not control our life.

The next series of questions is designed to help you explore your own anxious thoughts and fears and to determine which direction you are pulled: toward or away from God. As you reflect on each question, ask yourself if the fear or anxiety you feel brings you closer to God, or does it somehow interfere with God's plan for your life (see Proverbs 12:25; 29:25)?

Reflection Questions: A Look in the Mirror

Remember to observe as thoughtfully and accurately as possible, without judging your response. The goal is to gain insight into your growth and future choices and responses to life's circumstances.

1. Do I avoid doing things God wants me to do because of my fear and anxiety?
2. Am I anxious about speaking to others regarding their relationship with God?
3. Do I have a healthy fear and respect of God or a paralyzing fear?
4. Do I keep myself from doing things because I lack trust in God?
5. Will I take steps to face things I am anxious about?

6. If God called me to go to some place, would I be obedient and go?

7. Do I trust in the Lord to give me what I need—especially peace in my life—and allow Him to take away my anxiety and fear?

8. Am I anxious or fearful about tomorrow and what it will bring?

9. Do I avoid relationships because of anxiety and fear or what other people might think about me if they recognize the anxiety and fear that I have?

10. How is my relationship with God affected by my anxiety and fear, and what do I choose to do about this?

11. Do I avoid telling other people I am a Christian as a result of anxiety and fear?

12. If asked by God through someone, would I give my testimony in front of my church, or would I be blocked by my anxiety and fear?

Activity Suggestions

1. Select one or more of these questions now and respond in journaling.

2. Single out several questions that impact you, and discuss them with a trusted friend.

3. Search the Scriptures for promises that address your particular fear, and write them down. Use three-by-five cards, and post each one with the Scripture as a reminder to you that you can overcome this fear. Be sure to write down the date and circumstance as God clearly reveals to you how you are overcoming this fear.

Anger and Frustration

Anger, like a fire, is useful and beneficial but only when thoughtfully employed. When fire is controlled, managed, and channeled, it is a powerful tool in industry, and our home, but out of control it is a storm of damage and destruction. Anger has that kind of power. Under control, it is a motivator to work on unhealthy interactions and create helpful boundaries. However, in its most extreme misuse, anger becomes a flamethrower, devastating every relationship in its path, especially our relationship with God. Many will read this who are genuinely perplexed as to why their relational world is blackened and smoldering. My prayer is that as you read this, it will bring helpful insight so that you can move toward God in this area of your life.

A child's family, regardless of how dysfunctional, becomes their norm. Even when the family system includes abuse, a child might think, "That's just the way things are." Because their family is all they know, children may see it as "normal" or even their own fault. As a therapist I have felt sad and angry over these situations; this is righteous anger that God will also feel. But let's say that you were such a child—defenseless, vulnerable, deeply hurt—and now, years later, the anger burns, and as it smolders, it robs you of the very things you long for most: your relationship with God.

Anger is often triggered from our past, and unresolved, it grows over the years. Unresolved, our past hurts will control our lives and steal our future. God's wish for you is to work through the past and to reduce and release your anger in constructive ways.

Dealing with our historical anger and confronting the reasons for it will open the way to receiving the peace of God and getting back our control of present moments and dreams for tomorrow. Are you able to reflect on your hostile feelings in an objective way? Do they have a place that's healthy and helpful in your relationships? The questions below will help you evaluate whether your anger and frustration have become a distraction to finding God's peace and joy.

Questions on Anger to Consider

1. Do I get frustrated or angry at the simplest of things?
2. If I get angry, do I have a hard time letting go and calming myself down?
3. Do I try to understand the reason for my anger?
4. Do I let day-to-day frustrations build up to constant anger?
5. How quickly do I get angry with those I love most?
6. Have I caused damage to physical things around me because I was angry?
7. Have I injured people physically and emotionally because of my anger?
8. Have other people told me I need to seek help with anger management?
9. When I am driving, do I let other drivers frustrate me when they tailgate or go slow in the fast lane?
10. How do my childhood experiences affect my frustration and anger levels today?
11. Have I given my anger up to God and committed myself to changing?

Practical Steps

Did your responses to any of the questions surprise you? If you answered yes to one or more of these questions, then you have work to do. You may well be aware of your anger issue, uncertain how to proceed or change. Let me encourage you to find a supportive anger management group so you can have accountability during the recovery process.

Keep an anger journal for one month. Be sure to include the circumstances where your anger was unmanaged. What will you choose when a similar circumstance comes up again? If you are repeating the same old patterns, then your anger is interfering with your relationship with God and the future that is in His heart for you.

CHAPTER 10

OVERCOMING SADNESS, GRIEF, AND LONELINESS

From the therapist's chair: He anxiously paced in the waiting room, tattooed from head to toe, his six-foot frame filling my office doorway. "Surely this isn't my next client," I said to myself. Rarely am I concerned for safety, but my five-foot stature barely came to his waist. He told me he needed help with his anger. He had been arrested many times for barroom fights, and his family had had enough. He was a victim of severe childhood abuse, struggling every day with depression and grief over the lost childhood and bad decisions he had made in his own life. He wanted to know why he was so angry all the time. The counseling began, and to his surprise he uncovered deep feelings of hurt, vulnerability, and loneliness. The anger, a cushion of protection for hurt feelings, began to fall away.

Have you come to a place in your life where sadness and depression interfere with your relationship with the Holy Spirit and perhaps with everyone around you? Is the self in the middle of your circle continuously and consistently pierced with arrows of sadness and grief? We all have experienced losses and grief in our lives. Although it can be hard, processing through the grief will lead to understanding the losses. We do have to be aware that sadness can become intense and develop to the place where it has taken over. If we suppress the sadness, it can turn to ugly bitterness.

From Bev: "Many years ago I began to notice a difference in Murl's clients in the waiting room as compared with another therapist's clients. Although all had similar backgrounds and issues, Murl's clients were able to smile, laugh, and uncover and deal with their issues because they had hope—hope that they were capable enough and strong enough to make changes in their lives with guidance from the Holy Spirit. This hope through the Holy Spirit gave them the strength to move forward. Yes, it will be hard work, but the rewards will be life-changing and well worth your effort."

There are some great resources for you to explore. Many helpful books have been written on the process of grief and loss. Seek a grief recovery group, find a mentor, or I also recommend individual counseling. Draw out a loss line with the date of the event above the line and what emotions you experienced or stuffed listed below the line. This will allow you to see where further work is needed. Commit these difficult losses to prayer on a daily basis; wake up each morning with expectation to see how the Holy Spirit will direct you in finding peace that day.

Ask yourself these questions to clarify which losses you might need to explore further:

1. Do I have a hard time expressing sadness or grief?

2. Does sadness or grief become so strong that it takes over my life and pierces my very self?

3. Does a present loss or grief connect me strongly to past grief?

4. How does God want to help me when I do experience grief and sadness? Do I listen to what God has for me?

5. Have sadness and grief caused me to be bitter and angry with God?

6. Have loss and grief caused me to be bitter and angry with other people?

7. Do I know how to work through my losses and the grief that accompanies them?

8. Can I also have the joy of the Lord while I am experiencing sadness?

9. When I see the direction of our country and world, do I feel what Jesus felt when he looked over Jerusalem?

10. If someone else is experiencing sadness and grief, do I know how to comfort and come alongside them?

Sadness and grief are natural aspects of life and loss. As children we may experience great grief at the loss of a puppy or another animal. As we learn to express our grief and loss, the intensity fades, which enables us to better manage the loss. We will always have the memory of the loss, but it will no longer affect us so strongly. As we are able to release the sorrow in healthy ways, it does not turn into bitterness or blame. When individuals grow beyond their blame and bitterness, they can transform it into peace and joy through the Holy Spirit.

When we are most actively reflecting the character of God, we will find a freedom to experience these powerful emotions without being controlled by them. Getting to that place is a process, although we will never arrive at total completeness in this life. By listening to the Holy Spirit, we will be aimed in God's direction. Here are some Scriptures for further exploration: Psalm 37:39; 51:10-12; Proverbs 15:13; Hebrews 12:15.

CHAPTER 11

THOUGHTS AND THINKING
AS INTERFERENCES

I stood frozen against the instant chill in the room; gripping the phone, thoughts racing and flooding through my mind. It was the phone call no one wants to get, a sudden death. My mother had been killed— minivan versus 470-ton freight train, outcome obvious. She was on the way to Sunday school, Bible on the seat next to her, and then in a second she was with Jesus, learning from the Master. No one really knows why she was stuck on the track, most likely frozen in fear. My thoughts raced: I had an all-church fall kickoff dinner, I was hosting a table that night, I had a full week of clients, airlines, call the airlines, call my children. Pray, I should pray. Thoughts out of control, I became frozen in the moment.

Our thoughts are really an internal dialogue, which can benefit or interfere and lead us into problems. I eventually started breathing again and making lists and put my thoughts back into sequence. Some people do not stop to think; their thoughts either lead them closer to God or become a distraction or possibly a wall against the

Holy Spirit's work in their life. Do you continue to think like a child, forgetting to put away childish things (1 Corinthians 13:11)? Or have you developed your thought patterns so they lead you to wisdom and discernment (Proverbs 14:15; 21:29)?

The first question we need to ask ourselves regularly is "Where are my thoughts leading me?" but that's only a first step. Stop and ask yourself these questions:

1. Where are my thoughts leading me?
2. Do I do life without thinking, allowing my thoughts to interfere with life?
3. Do I think through alternatives for the best choice before speaking or taking an action?
4. Are my thoughts clouded by circumstances?
5. Are my thoughts easily influenced and led by the outside world?
6. Are my thoughts so fast that they confuse me?
7. Are my thoughts thorough, loving, and directed toward good decisions?
8. Do I think about other people before I speak or take action?
9. Are my thoughts in sequence or just random?
10. Do I use Scripture to consider and think through life's issues?
11. Am I able to tell when my thoughts are a direct attack against God's direction?

Two-year-olds don't think; usually they react on impulse. When adolescents are developing their thinking process, peers or circumstances often distract them. Non-thinking behavior is not beneficial to adults. In counseling sessions, I have seen far too many forty-year-olds whose thoughts are immature, addictive, and often destructive. In our relationship with the Holy Spirit, we need to stop the interference of our thoughts—those arrows that pierce through our mind so loudly we cannot hear His voice. Our thoughts can direct us to a close and intimate relationship with God as we learn to redirect our negative and unhealthy thinking back to God.

Right now, stop and review where your thoughts have been in the last couple of hours. As we review our thoughts, we are also developing more "self-observer" characteristics. A process called "thought stopping, thought control" uses a technique of paying close attention to our thoughts as they occur, actually stopping and evaluating them, and then redirecting them. For example, when you think about your boss, are your thoughts negative and lead you away from how God would want you to respond, or can you stop and redirect those thoughts to positive observations and responses?

Awareness of our thoughts will continually help our brain develop over our lifetime. Individuals who have suffered abuse sometimes find it difficult to manage their thoughts, partially because of their unresolved anger and other feelings. Writing down their thoughts, and then evaluating whether these thoughts are constructive or destructive, are beginning steps to managing their thinking.

As a Man Thinketh, So Is He, a book written by James Allen in 1905 and recently republished, really started me thinking what a profound truth it is. If we allow negative, self-destructive thoughts to control our thinking, our lives are going to be self-destructive, addictive, and controlled by every whim that comes along. We have to stand firm in stopping the interference that our thoughts create. We recommend reading Daniel Amen, researcher and author of many books such as *Making a Good Brain Great* (2005) and *Change Your Brain, Change Your Life* (1998).

CHAPTER 12

IS YOUR PAST AN INTERFERENCE TO GROWTH?

Have you ever read about or personally met an individual who has overcome a painful, often abusive past? I have met many brave and incredible individuals, both male and female, who through diligent hard work have set their past behind them—not forgotten, but transformed into positive and productive tools in their present. The past can be a troubling part of our life, or we can choose to process through the past and release the power it has over us. We may try to forget the past or bury it deep, only to have it surface again to cause problems in the present.

We learn patterns of behavior from our past, behaviors that are no longer beneficial and potentially harmful to others and ourselves. Working through our past in healthy, constructive ways will allow us to understand why we make the choices we are making in this moment. An unresolved past will have dire consequences in our future and hinder God's plan for our lives. A more resolved past could open up our future in amazing ways!

Like a video recording, our brain stores past experiences in several ways: visual and auditory memories, feelings, pain, tactile sensations, smells, sequences, and repetitions. One experience might be stored in a variety of ways within several of these categories. We might remember a fragment of the experience but not all the pieces. We might remember what led up to a traumatic event but store memories of the actual event in other areas of our brain.

> It happens every fall as the weather cools, the smell of smoke drifting across the highway on my drive home, the memories flooding back. So many years ago, yet the memories are vividly real. In the summer of 1968 my two-year-old son, my two cousins, and I had just taken water to my brother who was swathing a hay field in rural Merced County. Suddenly and without warning the car died, stopping on a tilted right embankment. I smelled smoke and opened the driver's door (which instantly shut), and immediately flames came up over the entire left side of the car. I couldn't reach my son, or the cousins. Yelling quite hysterically I am sure, I told the cousins to grab my son and run; they did just before the loud explosion. The car fire and explosion was so intense it melted the entire inside of the car; nothing remained. The fire burned a farmer's field and trees, and though I was scared, we were unhurt except for the awful smell in my nose, which seemed to last forever. Years later I catch myself on those fall days, thinking "Is the car on fire?" The stored memory is still so strong!

Our past can distort our perception as we continue to view and understand the circumstances of life. As we develop a mature self-observer, we begin to believe that understanding our past can be a tool to make better choices today. Actually, learning from the past is essential; otherwise, the same behaviors will repeat themselves again and again.

A first step toward an awareness of past patterns is writing them down, both problem patterns and beneficial patterns of behavior. For one week, at the end of each day make a list of the things you see as a pattern. Ask yourself, "Is this pattern beneficial or problematic?" In fact, here is a list of questions to consider:

1. How does my past affect me today?
2. When I look at my past, do I see progress and development, or does the past continue to interfere with the present?
3. Can I remember my past and know that I am eternally forgiven?
4. Do I dwell on the past with unhealthy thoughts and feelings?
5. Do I remember the way other Christians have treated me in the past with joy or with sadness?
6. Can I look to the past and see God's hand in my life from the beginning?
7. Do I stay so busy in the present that I do not have to remember the past?
8. Do I use God's Word to guide me to evaluate the past?
9. Do I use my experiences and what I have learned to help others who might be struggling?
10. Do I keep making the same mistakes again and again without learning from my past?

Ask God to help you become aware of where your past is distorting your present and how the past has kept you stuck in developing beyond your history. Once you have identified a pattern of behavior that needs changing, use your skills in alternative thinking to generate solutions to your behavior. Remember, there is always more than one way to respond to a past memory that might be controlling your feelings, thoughts, and actions.

Please understand that we want to encourage you, especially those of you who have unimaginable abuse (physical, emotional, mental, and sexual) in your past, to seek a trusted therapist, counselor, or group setting where you can develop healthy and constructive patterns. We desire for you to grow into a healthy and guilt-free life in the present. You can grow beyond the past!

CHAPTER 13

OUR PRESENT, TODAY

"This is the day the Lord has made; let us rejoice and be glad in it" (Psalm 118:24). Easier said than done, especially on a daily basis. I just have to either stop and pray or LOL (laugh out loud) when young mothers that I have the privilege of mentoring post that their three children are sick with only one bathroom, and I am sitting comfortably in my rocking chair on the covered deck watching my dogs play. We all have different circumstances, and whatever the circumstances are we need to remember that every day we want to show our love of God to others. Today is really a moment-by-moment awareness of our thoughts, feelings, and behaviors. Today also helps puts the past into perspective and provides a hope for tomorrow. What is it about today that helps you put the past into perspective and provide hope for tomorrow? For me, it is an awareness of God's presence.

From Murl: "I woke up this morning with serious pain in my left knee. I played far too many basketball games on hard court surfaces when I was younger. In spite of this, my question still remains: 'What would the Lord want me to do today?' Bev had an appointment at the office this morning, so I need to take care of our two dogs, one a fourteen-week-old puppy. After getting the dogs fed and out on their walk, my knee began to feel better. So again I asked myself the same question, 'What would the Lord want me to do today?' I decided to work on some copyright information for the book and proceeded to the computer. I realized that even in the normal, sometimes mundane daily activities; I need to be checking in with the Holy Spirit for direction. How do you find yourself asking for direction from the Holy Spirit during the day?"

Randy Alcorn, in his book *Heaven*, asks an important question: "In light of eternity how have I lived today?" I have changed this somewhat to ask myself, "In light of eternity, what choices have I made or will I make for the Lord today?" I know when I start my day with this question, I will consider my choices much more thoroughly. God has a plan for our days, and if we just put our feet on His pathway, it is not so difficult to follow His plan for the day. The stress of the job, the demands of sick children and others, the confusion of decisions to make, and the desire for prideful recognition become only momentary considerations in light of eternity.

Ask yourself the following questions as you journal about your today:

1. Am I thankful for today?
2. Do I need to break a bad habit starting today?
3. Did I experience the presence of the Lord today?
4. Lord, what do you want me to learn today?
5. Have I been stuck in a pattern of behavior today?
6. Can I look at today and see wise choices and maturity in those choices?
7. What questions do I need to ask myself about today?
8. Was God glorified in my life today?

9. Did other people see me act in the flesh or act in a godly way today?

10. Was today so busy that I did not even think about how I reacted or responded to my circumstances?

11. If I were to see the Lord today would He say, "Well done, thou good and faithful servant"?

12. At the end of today will I have peace about the way I spent these precious moments?

13. Will those I love know that I love them at the end of today?

14. Did I guard my tongue today? If not, from whom do I need to ask forgiveness?

The question becomes "How do we actually spend our time each day, and how would God want us to spend the time He has given to us?" Time is a precious gift of God, one that cannot be retrieved or saved.

Take one day a week and at the end of the day make a circle representing the twenty-four hours of that day. Ask yourself, "Where did I spend the last twenty-four hours?" Then divide the circle to represent the time spent on each activity. Maybe you spend time reading, exercising, watching a movie, or texting. Or maybe you washed so many loads of clothes that you lost count. None of these things are wrong and some quite necessary; but remember, we cannot retrieve spent time.

This exercise helps us with the development of our self-observer. Even while writing, I now realize I chose to complete my list of things to be done instead of playing with the children or watch a movie with them. Today when I see young moms taking the time to interact with their children, I know they have chosen wisely. It is my prayer you will reflect on how the present might be an interference with God's plan for you today.

Here is some Scripture talking about the present that you might consider:

> You have made my days a mere handbreadth; the span of my years is as nothing before you. Each man's life is but a breath. (Psalm 39:5)

> Do not boast about tomorrow, for you do not know what a day may bring forth. (Proverbs 27:1)

> Therefore we do not lose heart. Though outwardly we are wasting away, yet inwardly we are being renewed day by day. (2 Corinthians 4:16)

> Encourage one another daily, as long as it is called Today, so that none of you may be hardened by sin's deceitfulness. (Hebrews 3:13)

CHAPTER 14

OUR FUTURE

Have you ever wanted to know what lies ahead for your future? How often do you get caught up in the anxiety of what might be or could be rather than live joyfully in the today? How often do you allow the thoughts of the future to be an interference with God's plans for today?

Bev and I lost our fathers in the same year, 1976. I had finished my master's degree from Fresno State University in 1972, and although I enjoyed the ten years with the Merced County Probation Department, I felt as if there was something more. We prayed and asked God to reveal His plans for us. I had earned a teaching credential on the college level, so we applied to many Christian colleges, but all the doors shut. We looked into serving at a newly developing ministry in England; again the doors closed quickly. As youth coordinators we had been involved in camping ministry for many years; so we started to apply to various camping opportunities on the West Coast. American Baptist Churches of Oregon asked us to come and interview for a position at Camp Arrah Wanna in Welches, Oregon. We did and fell in love with the setting and ministry. In three weeks we moved a household of belongings, two children, three dogs, and a cat.

God knows the past, present and future. We can make the best plans possible and have hope for the future, yet only God knows what will occur beyond this moment we are in right now. There are 140 Bible verses regarding hope; hope is about what we cannot see. How often do we become anxious about the future? God tells us not to worry for tomorrow (Matthew 6:34), and yet we can spend a great deal of time and energy worrying. We do have a tendency to become anxious about the future, especially if we have little control of the situation.

To go on with our story: We served in camp ministry for four years, when suddenly, through leadership changes with a new direction, it was time to seek God in finding out what He wanted from us. Literally one day, Bev opened up the newspaper and there was an announcement: Oregon Graduate School of Professional Psychology was now taking applicants for the fall term to begin a Doctorate in psychology program. Wow, a complete change of course.

I didn't say earlier that Bev had a word from the Lord early in our marriage that she would be married to a doctor. I was a postman at the time, so she just filed this away. Now, at the moment of reading this announcement, she knew this was the choice of action we would make. I applied and was accepted, and the journey began. After moving from camp into an unfinished house; driving the fifty-plus miles each way for classes, working on internships and at various agencies, finally, with lots of prayer, I opened the doors to Mt. Hood Counseling Services in 1985. What would have happened if we had said no to God's calling? If we had not trusted God for the future, instead allowing interferences to stop us, literally there would not have been more than thirty years of counseling practice and help to so many.

Spend some time asking yourself these questions:

1. Am I constantly planning for the future?
2. Am I so busy with today that I do not consider tomorrow?
3. Do I listen and recognize God's plan for my future?
4. Do I worry so much for tomorrow that I do not have joy today?
5. Do I consider how my actions today or yesterday affect tomorrow?
6. Is tomorrow so far away it is just a fog?
7. Do I have hope for tomorrow as I experience God's love?
8. Do I understand how the past and present affect tomorrow?
9. If I continue in my present financial patterns, how will that affect my future?
10. If God gives me many tomorrows, where will I want to be, and what do I want to do? Does this match God's plan for me?
11. If I could look at what the Holy Spirit has planned for my future, would I be joyous, fearful, or anxious?
12. Do I think about the future for those I love and spend my time and energy to move myself toward a godly future to be a model for them?
13. Will my future be filled with people I need to apologize to and make amends with?
14. If God gave me a vision of our world tomorrow as He does in the book of Revelation, how would that affect my life decisions today?

You may be asking, "How can I have a hope for tomorrow if I cannot see how God has answered my prayers in the past or blessed me today?" Maybe you feel your today has been so confused and distorted that you cannot even begin to hope for a better tomorrow. I strive to get up each day and commit that day to the Lord. I have no idea what the day will bring, but I receive comfort knowing that I have already committed the day to the Lord.

Take some time to look back in your own life and begin to see how truly God was in charge the whole time and directed you (sometimes softly, sometimes more sternly) into the person you are to become for the Lord. I am not sure that, if I had known all that God had in our future, I would have made the steps forward or backward. Maybe that's why God knows the future, and we do not!

CHAPTER 15

HOW CAN OUR CAREER, JOB OR OTHER ACTIVITIES INTERFERE WITH GROWTH?

Have you ever envied another person's career or job? Are you consistently comparing your successes with others? We often judge or elevate people to a higher status of success by what they do. The old saying, "Time is money," which monetizes the value of time, is often a stumbling block that interferes with how God would have us work. As we read Scripture, we learn that generally this is not how God has laid out the plan of work. Obtaining educational degrees and climb-up-the-ladder promotions does not make the person. I have seen people others would consider to have very low status jobs, and yet they work their job with praise to God.

Both Bev and I have had many jobs in our earlier years. First, as a teen, long before you needed permits, I sold items door to door. I had a daily newspaper route and worked at the local Spudnut Donut Shop. Bev worked at the National Dollar Clothing Store in high school. During college I worked for the U.S. Postal Service and Bev at a bank and real estate office. We were wage earners then, not giving much thought to the significance or meaning of a career. As therapists in private practice, we have, as Bev says, "sometimes counseled individuals for veggies and eggs," and yet there is significant meaning-making in our counseling with others.

So how does what we do interfere with our growth and relationship with God? How many males do you know believe their career is everything: their self-worth, their moneymaking successes, and the prestige of status? What about time commitment? Many people, especially men, put the majority of their identity in what they have accomplished at a job or career, rather than their identity flowing from their position in Christ. Their job gives them either significance and position or the opposite: a feeling of failure and inadequacy.

Take some time and consider how you view your work, your job, and your career. Ask yourself some of these questions?

1. Do I work and do things so that God is glorified?
2. Do I feel that whatever I do is not good enough?
3. Is my identity or significance based on what I accomplish?
4. When I meet people, is the first thing I tell them what job I have or the promotions and degrees I have earned? If yes, why?
5. If I am criticized about how I do something, do I immediately feel inadequate or ashamed?
6. Do I look for things to do, or am I satisfied, "complacent," about just sitting around?
7. Do I look for work, or do I just let others take care of me?
8. Do I rejoice in everything I set out to do, even if it is difficult or an unpleasant task?

9. Do I only do what in my own eyes seems right?
10. Does God bless what my hands produce or has He withheld blessings because of my disobedience.

Stop and consider. If you are not in the position where God wants you to be, what needs to happen to get you there? Advanced education, specific training, or maybe the courage to step out and move forward in God's plan for your life? Commit today to pray for and seek God's plan.

What if the things you are doing in your leisure time are not part of God's plan for your life? Think about how much time you are spending during your day at work, with your family or others, or just hanging out. Keep a monthly journal, and make a commitment to change those areas that are out of balance and interfering with your relationship with God.

CHAPTER 16

MATERIAL POSSESSIONS AS A INTERFERENCE?

The rich young ruler asked, "Teacher, what good thing must I do to get eternal life?" (Matthew 19:16), Jesus answer culminated, "Go, sell your possessions and give to the poor, and you will have treasure in heaven. Then come, follow me" (verse 21). "When the young man heard this, he went away sad, because he had great wealth" (verse 22). God never asked us to sell it all, but we did relocate to Oregon as part of God's plan for our lives. What if we had not been obedient and moved?

From Bev: "Expensive things are not as important to me as the sentimental value of the objects. I am embarrassed to say I still have many of my children's toys and keepsakes, which the grandchildren now enjoy. Murl and I have been considering downsizing and will need to make many choices about what to keep and what to part with. Only by God's grace will I be able to get through the process."

Often what matters is not the fact that we have things, but rather the attitude we have about them. Luke 12:34 says that "where your treasure is, there your heart will be also." I believe this is an area of great difficulty for many Christians. We want what the world has to offer; yet we become almost controlled by the quest to acquire things. And when is enough really enough? In America we are seeing the results of overspending, whether because of our own choices or because lending companies grant loans far beyond the reach of the borrower. The intense struggle seems to be leveling off, and yet individuals have lost their jobs and their homes, and their anxiety levels have increased greatly. When you are not able to pay the bills, how does your anxiety interfere with following God's plan for your life?

Spend some time and ask yourself these questions to help you determine whether you have a healthy concept about possessions or whether this is an area that needs more of God's attention and growth.

1. Do I remember some of the things I had as a child and how those memories have stayed with me?
2. Do I just have possessions, or have they become so important that they possess me?
3. Do I believe that what I have determines whether God is blessing me?
4. Do I overspend my resources and put myself into major debt to get what I want?
5. Am I so eager to get rich and prosperous that I lose out on what is really important, such as family, relationships, and God's will for my life?
6. Do I use my money and resources to bless others?
7. If God took away all my money and things, would I be mad at God?
8. Would I be willing to give up my things if God called me to be a full-time servant or missionary for him?

9. Do I give God thanks for the little things that I have and feel blessed with everything God has given me?

10. Do I allow my possessions and resources to interfere with my relationships with other people, especially those I love?

Balance is difficult in a culture that honors possessions and having what you want when you want it. Loss, especially sudden loss of possessions, can be extremely difficult. We had to consider this recently. We live in a deeply forested area, and a wildfire came within six miles of our home two years ago. As the smoke intensified, I began to make a mental list of what I would take or leave if ordered to evacuate. Photos, important papers, Bible and research work, artwork from mission trips to Africa and India, the original wolf paintings by an artist friend who has passed. Of course, the animals, and, and … I become quite overwhelmed with the whole process. Then the next year it was a flood that took the road out a mile and a half from our house. Again the same process took over my thinking.

Ask yourself as you stand in the middle of your favorite room: what would you take? A saying I often use when sharing with clients is "In light of eternity …" what's really important? My relationship with my Lord, that is the most important "thing" I have.

CHAPTER 17

PRIDE AND VANITY

Pride is an undue sense of superiority, and vanity is excessive personal pride, both of which are fruitless and often useless. Pride and vanity hurt relationships, creating an atmosphere where others feel inadequate and uneasy around us. Pride is one of the greatest interferences to growth and our relationship with the Lord. When people are not aware of the needs of others, they will focus primarily on who they are and what they believe they have accomplished. Pride keeps us separated from God with an attitude that says, "I can do this all myself," or "I don't need God to tell me what to do."

Jealousy seems to be a by-product of pride, especially if we think someone else has something we think is better than ours. We can become jealous of material things, relationships, education, and skills that others may have. If you are jealous of someone or what they have, you need to look more deeply into the problem of pride. Pride and jealousy will become stumbling blocks to growth in Christ. In fact, pride and jealousy will interfere with our spiritual, emotional, relational, and mental growth. Keep on the path of pride, and you will miss God's direction and blessings for your life.

From the therapist's chair: He sat across from me, defiant, frustrated, and boasting of his accomplishments. He made sure I knew how much he had done for his church and how they just did not appreciate it. The board of deacons had requested he go to counseling; they thought that his pride and arrogance were interfering with his abilities to shepherd the church. For a full forty-five minutes he went on and on, listing all his accomplishments. Then I spoke, almost in a whisper, "What do you think the Lord would say about your list of accomplishments?" He started to boast again, and again I said, "Do you think you will hear Him say, 'My good and faithful servant, enter,' when you get to heaven?"

He almost said, "Well, why wouldn't He?" but stopped in midsentence. Then he began to cry loudly, saying, "I don't like who I have become!" Now we could begin therapy.

There is a perilous balance between healthy self-awareness of the talents and gifts God has given us and the slippery slope of pride and vanity. Becoming a healthy self-observer is vitally important in maintaining this balance. Use the following questions as a measure of how you believe you are doing in the area of pride and vanity.

1. Do I view myself as better than others in any area of life? What area?
2. Do I brag about things I have, what I know, or what I have accomplished?

3. Am I quick to be critical of others or jealous because of what they have?

4. Do I need to have the best clothes, car, or electronics to impress others?

5. Do I buy the most expensive item to impress others?

6. Do I present myself as a title (for instance, Doctor) rather than as a person?

7. Do I need other people to look up to me and become distant when they do not?

8. Do I need to take substantial risks to prove myself to others?

9. Do I spend impulsively and, when all else fails, pray afterward about my actions?

10. Do I look down on others based on their income, age, clothing, or other external factors?

The key to dealing with pride and vanity is to humble ourselves. First Peter 5:6 (NASB) says, "Humble yourselves … that He may exalt you at the proper time." How much has God been involved in what He has allowed you to accomplish? I have had some profound experiences in my travels to India, where I was gifted with an opportunity to meet the bishop of Southern India. This individual displayed God-given qualities of service and humility. During our conversation, it was never about what he had accomplished, but what God has been able to accomplish through others.

Oh, I pray for that kind of humility and the willingness to be used by God in whatever way. Pray for that humility for yourself, and watch how God will work through you.

CHAPTER 18

HOW DO WE LET OTHER PEOPLE INTERFERE WITH OUR RELATIONSHIP WITH GOD?

We start our lives in relationship with others: our parents or perhaps our grandparents as the most significant caregivers. We grow and develop patterns of behavior as we watch other people. We love and connect with some or avoid others because of being hurt by them.

Our attitude toward other people is important. Jesus was clear: "Love your neighbor as yourself" (Matthew 19:19). We can be critical of others, or we can be a blessing to them. Other people can be so important to us that we are controlled by them, or we may be the ones who try to control others. How we relate to other people either brings us closer to God or becomes a barrier to our relating to God. Some of us may be so controlled by others that we fear and become anxious when we strive to trust in God's will for our lives. The opinion of others becomes so important that we cannot develop a love for God's will for our lives, especially if God's plan is different from that of the controlling individual. We must first be fully committed to surrendering to God's will; then our relationship boundaries will become balanced and healthy.

Answer the questions below to decide for yourself how balanced you believe you are in relationships with other people.

1. What is my attitude toward other people? Can I identify an unhealthy attitude?
2. Am I able to forgive others and as a result have a relationship with God and them?
3. Do I view others as much better or much worse than I am?
4. Can I risk being myself with other people, or do I become anxious and fearful?
5. Do I try to control or manage other people's actions?
6. Do I meet new people easily and comfortably, or do I avoid situations where I might meet new people?
7. Do I let other people determine what I do?
8. Can I speak for myself with other people and set healthy boundaries?
9. Do I become closer to God or farther from God when I relate with certain individuals?
10. Do I view people differently based on their status or wealth?
11. Would God tell me, "You have loved other people as you have loved yourself"?
12. Do I look at the physical appearance of others and make that the main focus of the relationship?

Our view of other people will determine whether we have a healthy and growing other-person perspective and whether our view interferes with our relationship with God. Our view of other people is also a good reflection of our view of ourselves. If we are critical of others, it is almost always because we are self-critical. I have seen many people grow in their development of maturity when they begin to work on their own relationships. When a person views his or her spouse with unconditional love, as Christ sees us with unconditional love, the relationship will become healthier and grow fuller. It is often said you only hurt or get hurt by those you love the most. Is that true for you?

To further develop in this area, take a moment and write down all the labels you believe about yourself; now stick them on you. Once you are covered with the labels, consider how many of these same characteristics are distorted when you view others? In other words, if we believe we are stupid or dumb, how often are we using this filter to see others? Maybe one of your labels is unworthy and unloved, do you believe that about others? To see others clearly, we must first take the plank from our own eye (Matthew 7:3–5).

CHAPTER 19

HOW DOES OUR BODY INTERFERE WITH OUR RELATIONSHIP WITH GOD

What is your first thought about your body? We often describe our physical body as being too short, too tall, too thin, or too heavy: "I am an athlete," or "I am out of shape." We compare our body to others: "She's in better shape"; "He must really work out." Most individuals will not think about their body as a dwelling place for the Holy Spirit as Ephesians 2:21–22, 1 Corinthians 6:15-20, or 1 Corinthians 3:16 describes.

Either we treat our body in a way that allows us to do what God would have us do, or we abuse our body so that we are unable to accomplish what God has planned for us. We may focus so much attention on our bodies that we exclude God. The opposite is also true: we may ignore our body rather than honoring what God has given to us. There needs to be a balance regarding our body by seeking healthy choices while not overly focusing on it. The food we choose to eat and drink, the healthy exercise or lack thereof, the cleanliness or lack of care we give our bodies all tell us something about how we are taking care of God's gift to us, His dwelling place.

As we grow chronologically older, we realize how temporary and structurally fragile the human body becomes. God guides us in maintaining a balanced and healthy perspective about our bodies as we age and mature.

The body and brain are very complex systems. The body has the capacity for muscle memory. For example, I learned to shoot free throws blindfolded to develop body memory and to keep from being distracted by visual cues. There is also a touch and tactile memory. Either of these can bring about a reaction before a thought or conscious awareness. What we see, hear, smell, touch, or taste may trigger a body memory, often about a hurtful or abusive situation from our past.

Consider how you view your body. Are you taking care of your physical body so you can experience God fully, or has your physical body become a distraction from experiencing God? Some major issues to consider are how you view food, how you exercise, the amount of sleep you get, brain activity, your sexual focus, and the general care you give your body. Do you seek medical attention when you have symptoms, or do you ignore them? Do you start an exercise program only to abandon it at the first sign of not reaching a goal? Are you consistently stressed out about things you have no control over? These are all very personal considerations. Start by answering the following questions:

1. What is my attitude toward my physical body?
2. Do I ignore my body, or am I overly focused on my body? Is there balance?
3. Do I allow my weaknesses to control my body?
4. Is the Holy Spirit able to use me as a result of how I take care of my body?

5. Do I think about what I eat, how much I exercise, or the amount of sleep I get as caring for God's dwelling place within me?

6. Has my body been so abused that I am unable to hear God?

7. Is my body so important to me that I spend all my time focusing on it?

8. In which areas of caring for my body would God encourage me? Is there an area He has told me I am obsessing over?

9. Am I so busy with life that my body gets ignored or stressed out?

10. How would God want to release me physically to serve Him?

11. Do I consistently compare my body to those of others, always falling short?

12. Can I be content with the body that God has given me and follow His plan for my life?

Wherever you find yourself today, stop allowing your body to interfere with your relationship to God. Become a good self-observer, and strive to understand when and what your body is saying to you. I have a personal example I want to share with you.

From Bev: "About twenty years ago I had a very intense counseling load and was busy with adult children at various stages of their lives. I also was in the midst of some fairly complex premenopausal symptoms. I did not want to disappoint my clients or be unavailable for my kids. I can say today I was stressed out on many fronts.

"Someone decided they no longer wanted their aquatic frogs so they placed several of them in our large office salt-water tank. Next morning the frogs were all dead, and all of our beautiful fish had become floating slim. Without thinking (did you hear that?), with a very quick reaction I began to clean out the tank, without gloves! It took several hours to clean and dismantle the tank; done, or so I thought.

"Some weeks later I began to get a growth on my right wrist that became quite large. The doctor thought it might be a common ganglion cyst, and I was scheduled to have it removed. The growth was sent out for testing (which came back as questionable but not cancer), and within one week five more cysts were growing around the same wrist, with intense pain up my arm. After more surgery and lots of intense testing, samples were sent to an infectious disease specialist, who ruled the growth to be *Mycobacterium tuberculosis marinum*. The frogs were bad, but I was fortunate per the specialist, who said I could have lost my whole right arm due to the infection.

"So what did I learn from all this? Don't have frogs; don't clean bad water without gloves, and God wants me to take care of myself. I must not get so stressed out that I cannot think and make a clear plan. And stop and pray about every situation."

For the past couple of years Bev has had the privilege of being involved in two conferences in connection with Pure Desire Ministries, an effective ministry dealing with sexual addiction and the betrayal that occurs in families when a strong negative foothold of sexual perversion occurs. What is your belief about your sexuality? What are the lies you believe? Ask yourself these questions to further determine how you might be stuck:

1. Does my attitude toward sexual issues interfere with my relationship with God?
2. Am I dealing with guilt or shame issues over past sexual experiences?
3. Do I constantly have thoughts of a sexual nature that invade my mind's ability to stay focused?
4. When I look at a person of the opposite gender, where do I focus my attention?
5. Am I involved in a sexual addiction such as pornography or affairs?
6. Am I sexually avoidant because of what I believe about my body?
7. How do I understand God's attitude toward sexual issues?

If we allow our body to become a distraction to our relationship with God, we are going to be discontent with ourselves. We will not have the joy and peace that a genuine and authentic relationship with God can bring.

CHAPTER 20

WHAT IS NEXT?

I have been asking myself, "What is next?" for some time. Do we just end the book with the interferences with our relationship with God? Do we dig any deeper?

In the beginning we introduced you to SOCA, then described each in detail. How are you growing in each of these areas—self-observer; other-person-perspective; consequential thinking, and alternative thinking? Have you mastered any of these yet? No, neither have I; that is the beauty of growth to maturity. We have a whole lifetime of learning ahead of us.

Then we shared the seven stages of moral development. Where do you believe you are in the stages? Have you made a plan of growth to continue on maturing into the next stage of development? My favorite area to share has been the three diagrams of entanglement: the non-Christian, messy boundaries, and healthy boundaries, and of course the areas of interference that keep us stuck acting out the same patterns over and over again.

As we come to the end of this book journey, we both wanted to leave you with hope for the future and encouragement for today. We realize that in our world today, life is just hard, really hard for many of you. It is hard to think about maturity and growth when you are working two jobs just to stay afloat.

Let me encourage you to keep up the journey of growth and maturity, to finish strong, and never, never to give up. You can do this because you have an awesome, mighty, and unconditionally loving God who cares so much for you that He sent His son to pay the price so that you might have eternal life. With that said, I would like to share two other short pieces to this life puzzle: prayer; and peace and joy.

Prayer, Our Conversations with Our Father

It is difficult to have and maintain a friendship or relationship with anyone without having conversations with him or her. It is exactly the same in our relationship with God, our heavenly Father. We need to have conversations where we express ourselves to, share with, and petition God, as well as remain silent and listen to God. Praying is the moment-to-moment consideration of how we want to relate to our heavenly Father and certainly how He wants to relate to us.

> From Bev: When I pray, I don't use fancy words or well-worn phrases. I just let the Lord know that I am thinking about Him. I love to be out in nature and really have experienced some awesome moments given to me by my heavenly Father. I want to let Him know that I am excited about what He has allowed me to discover and usually, unless I am really excited, I will say, "Thanks, this is awesome." God is also the first person who hears from me when I am afraid or

need encouragement. I want prayer to be the language I use with my forever friend, Jesus.

From Murl: When I pray, sometimes I envision myself running toward the Lord. The closer I get, the more I am becoming like a little child, saying, "Abba, Father, I love you," and having Him wrap His arms around me and tell me, "I love you."

When do you pray? What do you pray for when you do pray? Are your words only patterns, or are they truly from your heart? God knows what is in our hearts long before we do, so what stops us from opening up our hearts to Him? From the beginning, in the garden of Eden, all God has wanted with us was the relationship of heavenly Father and child. Why are we so resistant to this relationship? When we really allow ourselves to be close to God, we realize this is the one relationship where we can trust, feel free to be who we are, and be forgiven. Yet we often choose the opposite—to pull away. What keeps you from drawing close to God?

Spend some time on the following questions, and then begin a prayer journal. Write down what you are praying for, and then write down how God has answered.

1. How often do I have conversations with God?
2. What is the focus of my prayers?
3. When I am praying, do I also listen to the Holy Spirit speaking to me?
4. When I pray in front of others, is it to impress them or just to talk to God?

5. Do I experience God's presence when I pray?

6. Do I allow my thoughts, feelings, and circumstances to interfere with my prayers?

7. Do I remember things God has done for me and give Him thanks?

8. Are my prayers just a well-established pattern, or am I having a conversation with God?

9. Do I see how God is answering my prayers?

10. Do I pray humbly for forgiveness and take responsibility for my actions

Towards Peace and Joy

Peace and joy are gifts from God. The Lord can offer them right in front of us, yet we may make the choice not to receive them. Our greatest joy is watching someone move from pain, depression, and anger toward peace and joy. Are you ready for the journey? We want to encourage you to continue on in the journey, and finish strong!

The Feeling Wheel

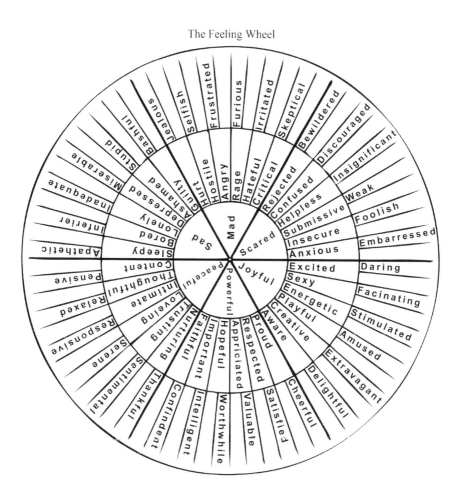

APPENDIX #1

What follows are two self-scoring questionnaires to evaluate areas of strength and areas for growth. Remember, this is about you; there is no right or wrong answer. Use this questionnaire as a guide to determine where you might want to focus your growth in right now.

Questionnaire for Emotional Interpersonal Development

Instructions:

Read each question below, thinking about how you behave or respond. How true is each statement about you? Respond with the numeric rating as follows:

4. If you regularly use this or do this
3. If you usually use this or do this
2. If you some of the time use this or do this
1. If you use this or do this a little
0. If you don't use this or do this at all

1. _____I am very aware of self and others before choosing a behavior, taking an action, or saying something.

2. _____I am aware of a full range of feelings (sad, happy, angry, peaceful, anxious, calm) but do not lose control of unpleasant feelings.

3. _____I have good boundaries between self and others while maintaining empathy.

4. _____I consider the consequences of actions and find the best alternative.

5. _____I consider my past as an aid to making decisions in the present.

6. _____I make adjustments in goals and behaviors based on changing circumstances without loss of integrity.

7. _____I maintain personal consistency in difficult circumstances.

8. _____I can disagree with others without making the difference into a problem.

9. _____I am seen by others as goal oriented with leadership qualities.

10. _____I can relate to others, no matter their age or status, in a loving, understanding manner.

11. _____I can be objective about myself recognizing my biases.

12. _____I am able to love myself, recognizing my sinfulness and weaknesses.

13. _____I am conscious of my thoughts before they become a direction or action.

14. _____I can be aware of my feelings and be sensitive to them without ignoring them or overreacting to them.

15. _____I am able to observe my thoughts and feelings before they become reactions.

16. _____I recognize my limitations and issues without being critical or judgmental of myself.

17. _____I can have a positive attitude about the future even when present circumstances are difficult and demanding.

18. _____I evaluate my motives for doing things before I do them.

19. _____I can look at my past decisions and actions taking responsibility for them without judgment that leads to guilt and shame.

20. _____I can manage my strong feelings so that I don't say or do something that I later wish I had not.

21. _____I listen and observe others to understand their intent, not just their words or actions.

22. _____I pay attention to the emotional significance of what the other person is saying or doing.

23. _____I ask questions to clarify if my understanding and interpretation of their intent is accurate.

24. _____Do I pay attention when others are talking to me, or is my attention on other things at the same time?

25. _____Do I observe the nonverbal cues that would help me understand the other person?

26. _____Do I let my biases override my objectivity and understanding of the other person?

27. _____Do I listen to the other person while still taking into consideration his or her age, culture, and frame of reference?

28. _____Do I listen for more than just the superficial level of the other person's words or actions?

29. _____Do I have a heart towards others when they are hurting me, and am I able to forgive them?

30. _____Do I listen to the whole message of the other person before I speak or jump to my conclusions?

31. _____Do I consider the benefits or problems of potential actions, including what I say?

32. _____Do I consider the circumstances, people, and culture involved in the present choice?

33. _____Do I stop myself from saying or doing things without considering the consequences?

34. _____Do I stop my biases or emotions from clouding my ability to evaluate my actions or words?

35. _____Do I deal with anxiety and fear about the future so they don't stop me from taking steps?

36. _____Do I consider the future in the long term or only see the consequences of the present time?

37. _____Do I slow down to consider consequences of doing things, or do I see the consequences only after they have happened?

38. _____Do I use past experiences to help in considering the consequences of my actions or words?

39. _____Do I guard my tongue so I do not say things before I consider them?

40. _____Do I consider what is leading my actions or words?

41. _____Am I objective in looking for alternatives, or do I become rigid or single-minded?

42. _____Do I let past successes or failures determine my alternatives (or do I stay open)?

43. _____Do I have the courage and believe in myself enough to come up with good alternatives?

44. _____Do I break old patterns and look for new alternatives?

45. _____Do I allow for creative alternatives?

46. _____Do I manage my thoughts and feelings so they don't block my alternatives?

47. _____Do I get stuck if there is more than one alternative to a choice?

48. _____Do I consider far enough ahead for my alternatives so that I don't just choose what is easier or more available?

49. _____Do I use wise people or material in looking at alternatives?

50. _____Do I ask questions of others to develop help with alternatives in what to do?

Add up your total score, and record that number in the box …

Scoring the Questionnaire

The group given this evaluation tool represents church leaders as well as young people, the age range being 16 to 73. The range of scores represented were from 97 to 179. The average score was 134. Inconsistencies may have occurred when an individual was either self-critical or had a high need to appear more mature. This is more of a tool to help individuals determine the areas in which they need developmental growth.

The first ten questions concern general development. The next ten questions are self-observing questions. The third set of ten questions deal with other-person perspective, and the fourth set of ten questions is about consequential thinking. Rounding things out, the last ten questions address alternative thinking.

Remember; do not use this evaluation as a means to be self-critical or critical of others. This is a tool to put in the toolbox to learn to evaluate your progress on the journey to maturity. Use it wisely, and you will continue to grow in your relationship with the Lord. We wish you the best journey possible.

APPENDIX #2

Some years ago a pastor asked me what I would ask someone seeking a leadership position in the church. I came up with these questions, some based on the process and stage of the person's development. You will want to use these questions wisely, not in a judgmental or critical format. Start by asking yourself these questions, and be transparent enough to share some of your answers with anyone you pose the questions to. This questionnaire works well in a group format:

1. How would you describe yourself? What else might you say about yourself?
2. What are the strengths you would bring if selected for leadership?
3. What difficulties would you have if selected as a leader?
4. How do you determine the best choices for the direction of the church?
5. What type of individual do you select as friends?
6. Have you experienced any church problems in the past, such as splits, death of a pastor, or conflicts between different groups in the church?
7. As a leader, how would you deal with these differences?
8. What do you use to help you in your development, spiritually as well as interpersonally?

9. How do you deal with criticism?

10. How do you deal with the stress and feelings involved in leadership responsibilities

11. If there were a camera in your home, what would the images say about your leadership style?

12. If the church chose to go in a direction different from what you think is best, what would you do?

13. How would you handle an individual in leadership who is involved in dishonest behaviors such as embezzlement, adultery, or physical or verbal abuse?

14. Do you believe the church body needs to be involved in major decisions? If so, what type of decisions?

15. What inconsistencies in your life might distract you from being a dedicated and sincere leader?

How Am I Doing, Lord? Survey?

Using a Likert Scale—(1) Rarely, (2) Occasionally, (3) Sometimes, (4) Weekly, or (5) Daily—how would you evaluate yourself on the following:

1. I read my Bible and apply it to my life.

2. I pray and praise the Lord personally.

3. I confess my shortcomings and my sins.

4. I am accountable to at least one person or small group in my walk with the Lord.

5. I put forth time and effort to serve the Lord.

6. I allow the Holy Spirit to flow through my life.

Add up your total score, and check out your total below:

25 or more	Flying high—living in a love life with God
18	Losing altitude and may not realize it.
14	Close to the ground and may crash
12 or lower	Flying blind—in trouble spiritually

Sources

Preface

1. Richard Krejcir, *Spiritual Maturity and Its Importance* (I Universe, 2008, www.churchleadership.org).
2. Viktor E. Frankl, *Man's Search for Meaning* (New York: Beacon Press, 1959, 1962, 1984). First Published in German in 1946.
3. *The NIV Study Bible, New International Version* (Zondervan Bible Publishers, 1973, 1978, 1984, 1985). All Scripture references in this book, unless otherwise noted.

Chapter 4—The C in SOCA

1. "O Be Careful, Little Eyes" (published in thirteen hymnals, 1950 to 1975. Also found at www.Lyricsofsongs.net).
2. JATO rocket car (Darwin Awards, 1995, also at www. darwinawards.com).

Chapter 5—The A in SOCA

1. "Risk Poem": Original author unknown. Mt. Hood Counseling Service, 1990.

Chapter 6—Research Basis for the Seven Stages of Development

1. James Fowler, *Stages of Faith* (Harper & Row, 1981).
2. Grant, Grant, and Sullivan, (1957, Public Domain)

3. California Youth Authority, California Department of Corrections and Rehabilitation, National Institute of Mental Health, *Development of Interpersonal Maturity.* This research is public domain, according to CDCR Research Department.

Chapter 7—What is Spiritual Development?
1. Steve Farrar, *Finishing Strong* (Water Brook Press, 1996).

Chapter 11—Thoughts and Thinking as Interferences
1. James Allen, *As a Man Thinketh, So Is He* (LN Fowler & Company 1905).
2. Daniel Amen, *Making a Good Brain Great* (Crown Publishing Group, 2005).
3. Daniel Amen, *Change Your Brain, Change Your Life* (Little Brown Book Group, 2008).

Chapter 13—Our Present, Today
1. Randy Alcorn, *Heaven* (Tyndale House, 2004).

Made in the USA
San Bernardino, CA
28 April 2020